Harriet G. Lerner, Ph.D., is a staff psychologist and psychotherapist at the Menninger Foundation. Her work on the psychology of women and on the management of anger and conflict has earned her national recognition among general and professional audiences. She received her B.A. from the University of Wisconsin, her M.A. in educational psychology from Teachers College of Columbia University, and her Ph.D. in clinical psychology from the City University of New York. Dr Lerner is a distinguished lecturer, consultant and workshop leader and publishes widely in scholarly journals and popular magazines such as *Cosmopolitan, Ms., Working Mother, Nation's Business* and *New Directions for Women*. She lives with her husband and two sons in Topeka, Kansas.

THE
DANCE
of
ANGER

A GUIDE TO CHANGING
THE PATTERN OF INTIMATE
RELATIONSHIPS

Thorsons

Thorsons
An imprint of HarperCollins*Publishers*
1 London Bridge Street
London SE1 9GF

www.harpercollins.co.uk

First published in the USA
by Harper & Row Publishers Inc.
First published in Great Britain
by Thorsons 1990
This edition 2004

24

A catalogue record of this book is
available from the British Library

ISBN 978-0-7225-3623-0

Printed and bound in Great Britain by
Clays Ltd, St Ives plc

MIX
Paper from
responsible sources
FSC™ C007454

FSC is a non-profit international organisation established to promote
the responsible management of the world's forests. Products carrying the
FSC label are independently certified to assure consumers that they come
from forests that are managed to meet the social, economic and
ecological needs of present and future generations,
and other controlled sources.

Find out more about HarperCollins and the environment at
www.harpercollins.co.uk/green

For my first family:

My mother, Rose Rubin Goldhor
My father, Archie Goldhor
My sister, Susan Henne Goldhor

And in memory
of my parents:

Henne Salkind Rubin and Morris Rubin
Teibel Goldhor and Benny Hazel Goldhor

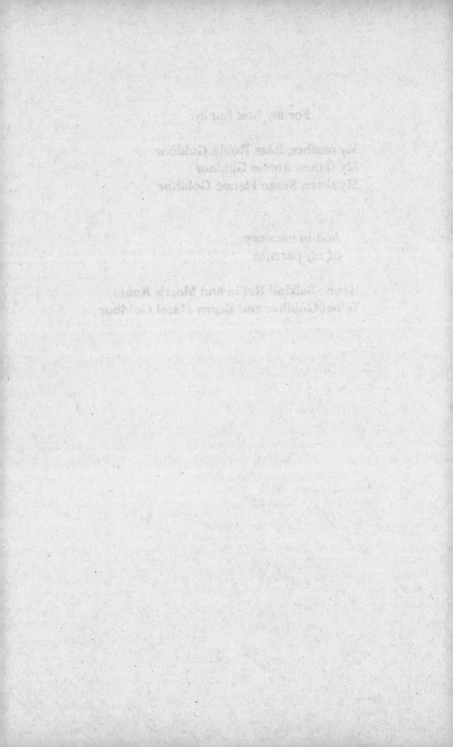

CONTENTS

CONTENTS

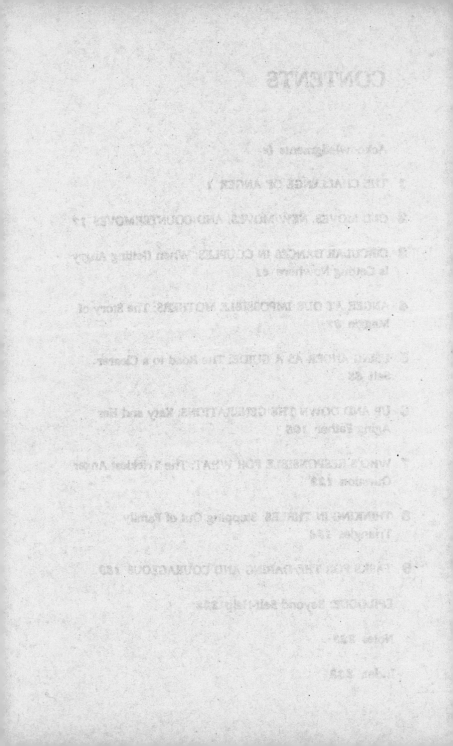

ACKNOWLEDGMENTS

I have many people to thank.

Sandra Elkin, my literary agent, steered me from professional to popular writing in 1979, and planted the seeds for this book. She saw me through an unanticipated series of literary ups and downs and demonstrated a remarkable capacity to maintain her sense of humor and clarity of direction, no matter what. Eleanor Rawson also helped me to develop as a popular writer by challenging my distant, scholarly style and encouraging me to connect more directly and personally with my readers.

In the early stages of this project, many friends and colleagues at the Menninger Foundation read manuscripts and offered valuable criticism and conversation. My thanks to Shirley Bonney, Nancy Gordon, Arthur Herman, Maria Luisa Leichtman, Arthur Mandelbaum, Sharon Nathan, Gavin Newsom, Dale Roskos, and especially to Meredith Titus. From outside of Topeka, Nancy Chodorow, Sally McNall, and Robert Seidenberg read chapters and offered feedback. While the bulk of my early writing did not find its way into the final version of this book, the feedback that I received from these people helped shape the course and direction of the final product.

Marianne Ault-Riché developed and named the "Talking Straight and Fighting Fair" workshops that we took on the road together as I gathered additional data about women and anger. Observing Marianne in action was inspirational to me; what I learned from her—of content, spirit, and courage—is reflected in this book.

I owe much to Sherry Levy-Reiner who carefully read and re-read chapters at the shortest notice, giving generously of time that she did not have. In addition to her vital suggestions, she offered me emotional support and feminist companionship at the Menninger Foundation, until her departure in 1982. I am similarly indebted to Emily Kofron whose loving friendship, camaraderie, and belief in my work nourished me through the good and bad times.

Katherine Glenn Kent has been, as always, an unfailing source of new ideas, which she translates with stunning lucidity and imagination into clinical technique. She introduced me to Bowen Family Systems Theory and helped me to put it into practice in my own life. What I have learned from her over our many years of friendship is incalculable, although I suspect that she would credit Murray Bowen with as much vigor and enthusiasm as that with which I now credit her.

Betty Hoppes typed the bulk of this book and worked second hardest next to myself. In addition to her outstanding secretarial skills, her support, wisdom, and generosity of spirit helped see me through. Thanks also to Mary McLin, who helped with the typing of early final drafts and to Aleta Pennington, Debi Smith, and Jeannine Riddle, who worked magic with the word processor.

I could not have written this book had I not been relieved of other professional responsibilities. I am grateful to the Menninger Foundation for supporting part-time employment and for making it possible for me to pursue my own work. My particular thanks to Donald Colson, Leonard Horwitz, and Irwin Rosen. Thanks also to Roy Menninger, president of the Menninger Foundation, for his generous encouragement and support of my activities.

Under the superb direction of Alice Brand, the professional library at the Menninger Foundation is nothing short of a scholar's dream. The library staff has retrieved all my requests with accuracy and expedience, and, in addition, has sent me numerous references that I did not request, but should have. The Menninger Library staff may be guilty of making it impossible for me to ever leave Topeka.

Janet Goldstein, my editor at Harper & Row, joined this project in its latter stages and proved to be everything that a writer could wish for. Her suggestions and criticisms were so clear, helpful, and wise, that the final rewriting of this book was ... well, almost fun. It is a blessing that my manuscript ended up in her gifted and enthusiastic hands. Susan Philipson did an excellent job copyediting the final manuscript.

There is no way that I can adequately acknowledge or name the influence of my parents in shaping my life and writing. I thank my mother for her warmth, her intelligence, her quiet dignity and courage, her love of life and remarkable spirit of survival, and her capacity to give generously to others in even the most difficult of personal circumstances. I thank my father for his wonderful humor and wit, for his appreciation of words and language, which he taught both his daughters, and for his loving, albeit unsuccessful attempts to steer me away from comic books and rock-and-roll during my formative years in Brooklyn. Finally, I thank my sister, Susan, for her correspondence and companionship, for her help with this project, and for being the very best of big sisters.

I wish also to thank the following people: My women's group for hand-holding and sympathy; Susi Kaplow for her pioneering article "Getting Angry"; Teresa Bernardez for inspiring the subject of this book and for being the most loving and demanding of critics; Judie Koontz for being such a good friend; Carol Tavris for providing long-distance, big-sisterly reassurance that this book would come out in my lifetime; Anthony Kowalski for having sensitively provided conditions for emotional and intellectual openness; Peter Novotny for encouraging my work all along; Susan Kraus for her special way of cheering me on; Ann Carver for reminding me through her gentle and graceful teaching of yoga that I cannot work and create as a disembodied spirit. I also want to thank the larger community of women, including many I have not met, who have reached out over long distances, even oceans, to encourage my ideas and to share their own. For this network, and for feminism itself, I will always stand in debt.

Last and most significantly, my love and gratitude goes to Stephen Lerner. He has been, along with everything else, the finest of editors, the best of friends, and the most nurturant of husbands. I thank him for his patience, his proddings, his all-around helpfulness and expert advice, for his seriousness as well as his irrepressible silliness. All this, combined with the bright faces and wonderful personalities of our two sons Matthew and Benjamin, have made me feel very lucky indeed.

This book, like others of its kind, is the product of many people's work. While I have tried in my Notes to acknowledge the specific contributions of others, those credited do not necessarily share my views. For example, I have used ideas and language from Bowen Family Systems Theory; however, my interpretation and application of Bowen's work has been heavily influenced by my psychoanalytic and feminist background. In sum, others have influenced this book, but the final responsibility throughout is mine.

The Dance of Anger

1

THE CHALLENGE
OF ANGER

Anger is a signal, and one worth listening to. Our anger may
be a message that we are being hurt, that our rights are
being violated, that our needs or wants are not being adequately met, or simply that something is not right. Our anger
may tell us that we are not addressing an important emotional
issue in our lives, or that too much of our self—our beliefs,
values, desires, or ambitions—is being compromised in a
relationship. Our anger may be a signal that we are doing
more and giving more than we can comfortably do or give.
Or our anger may warn us that others are doing too much
for us, at the expense of our own competence and growth.
Just as physical pain tells us to take our hand off the hot
stove, the pain of our anger preserves the very integrity of
our self. Our anger can motivate us to say "no" to the ways
in which we are defined by others and "yes" to the dictates
of our inner self.

Women, however, have long been discouraged from the
awareness and forthright expression of anger. Sugar and
spice are the ingredients from which we are made. We are

1

the nurturers, the soothers, the peacemakers, and the steadiers of rocked boats. It is our job to please, protect, and placate the world. We may hold relationships in place as if our lives depended on it.

Women who openly express anger at men are especially suspect. Even when society is sympathetic to our goals of equality, we all know that "those angry women" turn everybody off. Unlike our male heroes, who fight and even die for what they believe in, women may be condemned for waging a bloodless and humane revolution for their own rights. The direct expression of anger, especially at men, makes us unladylike, unfeminine, unmaternal, sexually unattractive, or, more recently, "strident." Even our language condemns such women as "shrews," "witches," "bitches," "hags," "nags," "man-haters," and "castrators." They are unloving and unlovable. They are devoid of femininity. Certainly, you do not wish to become one of *them*. It is an interesting sidelight that our language—created and codified by men— does not have *one* unflattering term to describe men who vent their anger at women. Even such epithets as "bastard" and "son of a bitch" do not condemn the man but place the blame on a woman—his mother!

The taboos against our feeling and expressing anger are s , powerful that even *knowing* when we are angry is not a simple matter. When a woman shows her anger, she is likely to be dismissed as irrational or worse. At a professional conference I attended recently, a young doctor presented a paper about battered women. She shared many new and exciting ideas and conveyed a deep and personal involvement in her subject. In the middle of her presentation, a well-known psychiatrist who was seated behind me got up to leave. As he stood, he turned to the man next to him and made his diagnostic pronouncement: "Now, *that* is a *very* angry woman." That was that! The fact that he detected—or thought he detected—an angry tone to her voice disqualified not only what she had to say but also who she was. Because the very possibility that we are angry often meets with rejection and disapproval from others, it is no wonder that it is hard for us to know, let alone admit, that we are angry.

Why are angry women so threatening to others? If we are guilty, depressed, or self-doubting, we stay in place. We do not take action except against our own selves and we are unlikely to be agents of personal and social change. In contrast, angry women may change and challenge the lives of us all, as witnessed by the past decade of feminism. And change is an anxiety-arousing and difficult business for everyone, including those of us who are actively pushing for it.

Thus, we too learn to fear our own anger, not only because it brings about the disapproval of others, but also because it signals the necessity for change. We may begin to ask ourselves questions that serve to block or invalidate our own experience of anger: "Is my anger legitimate?" "Do I have a right to be angry?" "What's the use of my getting angry?" "What good will it do?" These questions can be excellent ways of silencing ourselves and shutting off our anger.

Let us question these questions. Anger is neither legitimate nor illegitimate, meaningful nor pointless. Anger simply is. To ask, "Is my anger legitimate?" is similar to asking, "Do I have a right to be thirsty? After all, I just had a glass of water fifteen minutes ago. Surely my thirst is not legitimate. And besides, what's the point of getting thirsty when I can't get anything to drink now, anyway?"

Anger is something we feel. It exists for a reason and always deserves our respect and attention. We all have a right to *everything* we feel—and certainly our anger is no exception.

There are questions about anger, however, that may be helpful to ask ourselves: "What am I really angry about?" "What is the problem, and whose problem is it?" "How can I sort out who is responsible for what?" "How can I learn to express my anger in a way that will not leave me feeling helpless and powerless?" "When I'm angry, how can I clearly communicate my position without becoming defensive or attacking?" "What risks and losses might I face if I become clearer and more assertive?" "If getting angry is not working for me, what can I do differently?" These are questions that we will be addressing in subsequent chapters, with the goal, not of getting rid of our anger or doubting its validity, but of gaining greater clarity about its sources and then learning to take a new and different action on our own behalf.

There is, however, another side of the coin: If *feeling angry signals a problem, venting anger does not solve it. Venting anger may serve to maintain, and even rigidify, the old rules and patterns in a relationship, thus ensuring that change does not occur.* When emotional intensity is high, many of us engage in nonproductive efforts to change the other person, and in so doing, fail to exercise our power to clarify and change our own selves. The old anger-in/anger-out theory, which states that letting it all hang out offers protection from the psychological hazards of keeping it all pent up, is simply not true. Feelings of depression, low self-esteem, self-betrayal, and even self-hatred are inevitable when we fight but continue to submit to unfair circumstances, when we complain but live in a way that betrays our hopes, values and potentials, or when we find ourselves fulfilling society's stereotype of the bitchy, nagging, bitter, or destructive woman.

Those of us who are locked into ineffective expressions of anger suffer as deeply as those of us who dare not get angry at all.

ANGER GONE WRONG

If our old familiar ways of managing anger are not working for us, chances are that we fall into one or both of the following categories: In the "nice-lady" category, we attempt to avoid anger and conflict at all costs. In the "bitch" category, we get angry with ease, but we participate in ineffective fighting, complaining, and blaming that leads to no constructive resolution.

These two styles of managing anger may appear to be as different as night and day. In reality, they both serve equally well to protect others, to blur our clarity of self, and to ensure that change does not occur. Let's see how this works.

The "Nice Lady" Syndrome

If we are "nice ladies," how do we behave? In situations that might realistically evoke anger or protest, we stay silent—or become tearful, self-critical, or "hurt." If we do feel angry, we keep it to ourselves in order to avoid the possibility of open conflict. But it is not just our anger that we keep to ourselves; in addition, we may avoid making clear statements about what we think and feel, when we suspect that such clarity would make another person uncomfortable and expose differences between us.

When we behave in this way, our primary energy is directed toward protecting another person and preserving the harmony of our relationships at the expense of defining a clear self. Over time we may lose our clarity of self, because we are putting so much effort into "reading" other people's reactions and ensuring that we don't rock the boat, we may become less and less of an expert about our own thoughts, feelings, and wants.

The more we are "nice" in these ways, the more we accumulate a storehouse of unconscious anger and rage. Anger is inevitable when our lives consist of giving in and going along; when we assume responsibility for other people's feelings and reactions; when we relinquish our primary responsibility to proceed with our own growth and ensure the quality of our own lives; when we behave as if having a relationship is more important than having a self. Of course, we are forbidden from experiencing this anger directly, since "nice ladies," by definition, are not "angry women."

Thus begins a self-defeating and self-perpetuating cycle. The more we give in and go along, the more our anger builds. The more we intensify our repressive efforts, the more we unconsciously fear a volcanic eruption should we begin to let our anger out. So, the more desperately we repress . . . and so it goes. When we finally do "blow," we may then confirm our worst fears that our anger is indeed "irrational" and "destructive." And other people may write us off as neurotic, while the real issues go unaddressed, and the cycle begins again.

Although "nice ladies" are not very good at feeling angry, we may be great at feeling guilty. As with depression or feeling hurt, we may cultivate guilt in order to blot out the awareness of our own anger. Anger and guilt are just about incompatible. If we feel guilty about not *giving* enough or not *doing* enough for others, it is unlikely we will be angry about not *getting* enough. If we feel guilty that we are not properly fulfilling our prescribed feminine role, we will have neither the energy nor the insight to question the prescription itself—or who has done the prescribing. Nothing, but nothing, will block the awareness of anger so effectively as guilt and self-doubt. Our society cultivates guilt feelings in women such that many of us still feel guilty if we are anything less than an emotional service station to others.

Nor is it easy to gain the courage to stop feeling guilty and begin to use our anger to question and define what is right and appropriate for our own lives. Just at that point when we are serious about change, others may redouble their guilt-inducing tactics. We may be called "selfish," "immature," "egocentric," "rebellious," "unfeminine," "neurotic," "irresponsible," "ungiving," "cold," or "castrating." Such slurs on our character and femininity are perhaps more than many of us can bear. When we are taught that our worth and identity are to be found in loving and being loved, it is indeed devastating to have our attractiveness and womanliness questioned. How tempting it may be to shuffle apologetically back to our "proper place" in order to regain the approval of others.

Unlike the "bitches" among us, who are doomed to lose popularity contests—if not our jobs—"nice ladies" are rewarded by society. The personal costs, however, are very high and affect every aspect of our emotional and intellectual life. "See no evil, hear no evil, speak no evil" becomes the unconscious rule for those of us who must deny the awareness and expression of our anger. The "evil" that we must avoid includes any number of thoughts, feelings, and actions that might bring us into open conflict, or even disagreement, with important others. To obey this rule, we must become sleepwalkers. We must not see clearly, think precisely, or remember freely. The amount of creative, intellectual, and sexual energy that is trapped by this need to repress anger and remain unaware of its sources is simply incalculable.

The "Bitchy" Woman

Those of us who are "bitches" are not shy about getting angry and stating our differences. However, in a society that does not particularly value angry women, this puts us in danger of earning one or another of those labels that serve as a warning to silence us when we threaten others, especially men. Like the word "unfeminine" but even more so, these labels may have the power either to shock us into silence, or to further inflame us by intensifying our feelings of injustice and powerlessness. In the latter case, a label like "castrating bitch" can become a self-fulfilling prophecy.

But this is only part of the story. The negative words and images that depict women who do speak out are more than just cruel sexist stereotypes; they also hint at a painful reality. Words like "nagging," "complaining," and "bitching" are words of helplessness and powerlessness, which do not imply even the possibility of change. They are words that reflect the "stuck" position that characterizes our lives when a great deal of emotion is flying around and nothing is really changing.

When we vent our anger ineffectively, we can easily get locked into a self-perpetuating, downward cycle of behavior. We *do* have something to be angry about, but our complaints are not clearly voiced and we may elicit other people's disapproval instead of their sympathy. This only increases our sense of bitterness and injustice; yet, all the while, the actual issues go unidentified. On top of that, we may become a prime scapegoat for men who dread female anger and for women who wish to avoid their own.

Obviously it requires courage to know when we are angry and to let others hear about it. The problem occurs when we get stuck in a pattern of ineffective fighting, complaining, and blaming that only preserves the status quo. When this happens, we unwittingly protect others at our own expense. On the one hand, an angry woman is threatening. When we voice our anger ineffectively, however—without clarity, direction, and control—it may, in the end, be reassuring to others. We allow ourselves to be written off and we provide others with an excuse not to take us seriously and hear what we are saying. In fact, we even help others to stay calm. Have you ever watched another person get cooler, calmer, and more intellectual as you became more infuriated and "hysterical"? Here the nature of our fighting or angry accusations may actually allow the other person to get off the hook.

Those of us who fight ineffectively are usually caught up in unsuccessful efforts to change a person who does not want to change. When our attempts to change the other person's beliefs, feelings, reactions, or behaviors do not work, we may then continue to do more of the same, reacting in predictable, patterned ways that only escalate the very problems we complain about. We may be so driven by emotionality that we do not reflect on our options for behaving differently or even believe that new options are possible. Thus, our fighting protects the old familiar patterns in our relationships as surely as does the silence of "nice ladies."

We have all had firsthand experience with both of these self-defeating and self-perpetuating behavior patterns. Indeed, "nice ladies" and "bitches" are simply two sides of the same coin, despite their radically different appearance. After all is said and done—or *not* said and done—the outcome is the same: We are left feeling helpless and powerless. We do not feel in control of the quality and direction of our lives. Our sense of dignity and self-esteem suffers because we have not effectively clarified and addressed the real issues at hand. And nothing changes.

Most of us have received little help in learning to use our anger to clarify and strengthen ourselves and our relationships. Instead, our lessons have encouraged us to fear anger excessively, to deny it entirely, to displace it onto inappropriate targets, or to turn it against ourselves. We learn to deny that there is any cause for anger, to close our eyes to its true sources, or to vent anger ineffectively, in a manner that only maintains rather than challenges, the status quo. Let us begin to unlearn these things so that we can use our "anger energy" in the service of our own dignity and growth.

THE ROAD AHEAD

This book is designed to help women move away from styles of managing anger that do not work for us in the long run. These include *silent submission, ineffective fighting and blaming,* and *emotional distancing.* My task is to provide the reader with the insight and practical skills to stop behaving in our old predictable ways and begin to use anger to clarify a new position in significant relationships.

What Is the Focus of This Book? Because the subject of anger touches on every aspect of our lives, I have made some choices. In order to avoid writing an unmanageably fat volume, I have decided to focus largely, although not exclusively, on the family. We know our greatest anger, as well as our deepest love, in our roles as daughters, sisters, lovers, wives, and mothers. Family relationships are the most influential in our lives, and the most difficult. It is here that closeness often leads to "stuckness," and our efforts to change things only lead to more of the same. When we can learn to use our anger energy to get unstuck in our closest and stickiest relationships, we will begin to move with greater clarity, control, and calm in every relationship we are in, be it with a friend, a co-worker, or the corner grocer. Issues that go unaddressed with members of our first family only fuel our fires in other relationships.

What Is the Scope of This Book? I have written this book specifically with the goal that it be useful. I have sacrificed theory, no matter how interesting, if I did not think that it had a clear, practical application to the real lives of real women. Yet, in the process of writing about anger, I found that I not only had to narrow my subject; I also had to broaden it. The reader should be forewarned that this book does not lay out rules on "how to do it" in ten easy steps. This is because the ability to use anger as a tool for change requires that we gain a deeper understanding and knowledge of how relationships operate.

Thus, we will be looking at the ways in which we betray and sacrifice the self in order to preserve harmony with others ("de-selfing"); we will be exploring the delicate balance between individuality (the "I") and togetherness (the "we") in relationships; we will be examining some of the roles and rules that define our lives and serve to elicit our deepest anger while forbidding its expression; we will be analyzing how relationships get stuck and how they can get unstuck. We will see how close relationships are akin to circular dances, in which the behavior of each partner provokes and maintains the behavior of the other. In a nutshell, we can learn how to use our anger as a starting point to *change patterns* rather than *blame people*.

How Does One Make Use of This Book? Very slowly. No matter how crazy or self-defeating our current behavior appears to be, it exists for a reason and may serve a positive and protective function for ourselves or others. If we want to change, it is important to do so slowly so that we have the opportunity to observe and test out the impact of one small but significant change on a relationship system. If we get ambitious and try to change too much too fast, we may not change at all. Instead, we may stir up so much anxiety and emotional intensity within ourselves and others as to eventually reinstate old patterns and behaviors. Or we may end up hastily cutting off from an important relationship, which is not necessarily a good solution.

This book will be most useful if you read it all. Don't skip the discussions about children because you don't have kids, or the chapter on husbands because you are single or divorced. What is important is the relationship patterns that I will describe. The specific partners are less the issue than the form of the dance and how it works. Remember that each chapter contains information that has relevance for any relationship that you are in. As you read, you can generalize to other settings and relationships, and the exercise of doing so is a useful one.

In order to use our anger as a tool for change in relationships, we will be learning to develop and sharpen our skills in four areas:

1. *We Can Learn to Tune In to the True Sources of Our Anger and Clarify Where We Stand.* "What about the situation makes me angry?" "What is the real issue here?" "What do I think and feel?" "What do I want to accomplish?" "Who is responsible for what?" "What, specifically, do I want to change?" "What are the things I will and will not do?" These may seem like simple questions, but we will see later just how complex they can be. It is amazing how frequently we march off to battle without knowing what the war is all about. We may be putting our anger energy into trying to change or control a person who does not want to change, rather than putting that same energy into getting clear about our own position and choices. This is especially true in our closest relationships, where, if we do not learn to use our anger first to clarify our own thoughts, feelings, priorities, and choices, we can easily get trapped in endless cycles of fighting and blaming that go nowhere. Managing anger effectively goes hand in hand with developing a clearer "I" and becoming a better expert on the self.

2. *We Can Learn Communication Skills.* This will maximize the chances that we will be heard and that conflicts and differences will be negotiated. On the one hand, there may be nothing wrong with venting our anger spontaneously, as we feel it, and without intervening thought and delibera-

tion. There are circumstances in which this is helpful and those in which it is simply necessary—that is, if we are not abusive in doing so. Many times, however, blowing up or fighting may offer temporary relief, but when the storm passes, we find that nothing has really changed. Further, there are certain relationships in which maintaining a calm, nonblaming position is essential in order for lasting change to occur.

3. *We Can Learn to Observe and Interrupt Nonproductive Patterns of Interaction.* Communicating clearly and effectively is difficult even in the best of circumstances. When we are angry, it is more difficult still. It is hardly possible to be self-observant or flexible in the midst of a tornado. When emotions are high, we can learn to calm down and stand back a bit in order to sort out the part we play in the interactions that we complain about.

Learning to observe and change our part in relationship patterns goes hand in hand with an increased sense of personal responsibility in every relationship that we are in. By "responsibility," I do not mean self-blame or the labeling of ourselves as the "cause" of the problem. Rather, I speak here of "response-ability"—that is, the ability to observe ourselves and others in interaction and to respond to a familiar situation in a new and different way. We cannot make another person change his or her steps to an old dance, but if we change our own steps, the dance no longer can continue in the same predictable pattern.

4. *We Can Learn to Anticipate and Deal with Counter-moves or "Change back!" Reactions from Others.* Each of us belongs to larger groups or systems that have some investment

in our staying exactly the same as we are now. If we begin to change our old patterns of silence or vagueness or ineffective fighting and blaming, we will inevitably meet with a strong resistance or countermove. This "Change back!" reaction will come both from inside our own selves and from significant others around us. We will see how it is those closest to us who often have the greatest investment in our staying the same, despite whatever criticisms and complaints they may openly voice. We also resist the very changes that we seek. This resistance to change, like the will to change, is a natural and universal aspect of all human systems.

In the chapters that follow, we will be taking a close look at the strong anxiety that inevitably is aroused when we begin to use our anger to define our own selves and the terms of our own lives more clearly. Some of us are able to *start out* being clear in our communications and firm in our resolve to change, only to back down in the face of another person's defensiveness or attempts to disqualify what we are saying. If we are serious about change, we can learn to anticipate and manage the anxiety and guilt evoked in us in response to the countermoves or "Change back!" reactions of others. More difficult still is acknowledging that part of our inner selves that fears and resists change.

For now, let me say that it is never easy to move away from silent submission or ineffective fighting toward a calm but firm assertion of who we are, where we stand, what we want, and what is and is not acceptable to us. Our anxiety about clarifying what we think and how we feel may be greatest in our most important relationships. As we become truly clear and direct, other people may become just as clear and direct about their own thoughts and feelings or about the fact that they are not going to change. When we accept these realities, we may have some painful choices to make: Do we choose to stay in a particular relationship or situation? Do we choose to leave? Do we stay and try to do something different ourselves? If so, what? These are not easy questions to answer or even to think about.

In the short run, it is sometimes simpler to continue with our old familiar ways, even when personal experience has shown them to be less than effective. In the long run, however, there is much to be gained by putting the lessons of this book into practice. Not only can we acquire new ways of managing old angers; we can also gain a clearer and stronger "I" and, with it, the capacity for a more intimate and gratifying "we." Many of our problems with anger occur when we choose between having a relationship and having a self. This book is about having both.

2

OLD MOVES, NEW MOVES, AND COUNTERMOVES

The evening before my workshop on anger was scheduled to take place, a woman named Barbara telephoned me at home to cancel her registration. In a voice that conveyed both resentment and distress, she told me the following:

"I so much wanted to come to your workshop, but my husband put his foot down. I fought with him until I was blue in the face, but he won't let me come."

"What was his objection?" I inquired.

"You!" she said. "He said that you were a radical women's libber and that the workshop was not worth the money. I told him that you were a well-known psychologist and that the workshop would certainly be very good. I'm *sure* the workshop is worth the money, but I couldn't convince him of that. 'No' was his final word."

"I'm sorry," I said.

"Yes, so am I," she continued. "And I've had a terrible headache since then and a good cry. But I did put up quite a fight. In fact, my husband even agreed that I could use some kind of help with my anger because I behaved so badly."

I hung up the telephone and thought about the brief conversation that had just taken place. Clearly, this woman did not *have* to cancel her registration to the workshop. She could have chosen to do otherwise. She could not, however, have chosen to do otherwise without consequences. Perhaps the consequence that she feared was the loss of her most important relationship.

What is *your* reaction to the telephone conversation?

Do you think . . .
"Her husband is a real chauvinist!"
Or . . .
"What an insecure and frightened man."

Do you think . . .
"I feel sorry for this poor woman."
Or . . .
"This masochistic woman could sure use psychotherapy."
Or . . .
"Why didn't she pick herself up and go to the workshop!"

Do you think . . .
"He is to blame. How can he do this to her!"
Or . . .
"She is to blame. How can she allow him to make decisions about *her* life!"
Or . . .
"Society is to blame. How sad it is that we teach men to do this and teach women to take it."

Do you think . . .

"She is upset because her husband won't let her go to the workshop."

Or . . .

"She is upset because she is giving in."

Do you think . . .

"I can see myself in her."

Or . . .

"I can't relate to this at all."

We may each have our own personal reaction to what Barbara says. Many of us will not *want* to identify with her story. Yet, what she does, and how she feels, is far from outdated or unique:

She submits to unfair circumstances.

She does not feel in control of her life.

She has not effectively addressed the real issues at hand.

She is unclear about her own contribution to her dilemma.

She sacrifices her own growth to bolster and protect her husband.

She preserves the status quo in her marriage at the expense of her own self.

She avoids testing how much flexibility her marriage has to tolerate change on her part.

She feels helpless and powerless.

She turns anger into tears.

She gets a headache.

She does not like herself.

She believes that she behaves badly.

Are any of the above unfamiliar to you? Probably not. One or all of these things happen to us when we engage in ineffective fighting and blaming or when we are afraid to fight at all.

Unlike some women who dare not differ with their husbands, or lovers, Barbara has no problem getting angry. Her problem is that she fights in a manner that ensures that change will not occur and she *protects* her husband and the status quo of their relationship at the expense of her own growth. Carry on as she may, Barbara does not challenge the basic rule in the relationship—that her husband makes the rules. She "de-selfs" herself for her man.

What is "de-selfing?" Obviously, we do not always get our way in a relationship or do everything that we would like to do. When two people live under the same roof, differences inevitably arise which require compromise, negotiation, and give and take. If Barbara's husband was upset about the workshop, and if the workshop was not really that important to her, she might have decided to forget it. This in itself would not necessarily be a problem for her.

The problem occurs when one person—often a wife—does more giving in and going along than is her share and does not have a sense of clarity about her decisions and control over her choices. De-selfing means that too much of one's self (including one's thoughts, wants, beliefs, and ambitions) is "negotiable" under pressures from the relationship. Even when the person doing the most compromising of self is not aware of it, de-selfing takes its inevitable toll. The partner who is doing the most sacrificing of self stores up the most repressed anger and is especially vulnerable to becoming depressed and developing other emotional problems. She (and in some cases he) may end up in a therapist's office, or even in a medical or psychiatric hospital, saying, "What is wrong with *me?*" rather than asking, "What is wrong with this relationship?" Or she may express her anger, but at inappropriate times, over petty issues, in a manner that may invite others simply to ignore her or to view her as irrational or sick.

A form of de-selfing, common to women, is called "underfunctioning." The "underfunctioning-overfunctioning" pattern is a familiar one in couples. How does it work? Research in marital systems has demonstrated that when women and men pair up, and stay paired up, they are usually at the *same* level of "independence," or emotional maturity. *Like a seesaw, it is the underfunctioning of one individual that allows for the overfunctioning of the other.*

A wife, for example, may become increasingly entrenched in the role of the weak, vulnerable, dependent, or otherwise dysfunctional partner. Her husband, to the same degree, may disown and deny these qualities in himself. He may begin to direct the bulk of his emotional energy toward reacting to his spouse's problems, rather than identifying and sharing his own. Underfunctioners and overfunctioners provoke and reinforce each other's behavior, so that the seesaw becomes increasingly hard to balance over time. The more the man avoids sharing his own weaknesses, neediness, and vulnerability, the more his woman may experience and express more than her share. The more the woman avoids showing her competence and strength, the more her man will have an inflated sense of his own. And if the underfunctioning partner starts looking better, the overfunctioning partner will start looking worse.

My brief telephone conversation with Barbara suggests

that she is the underfunctioner in her marriage. Of course, not all women sit on the bottom of the seesaw in their relationships. In real life, there are any number of happy and unhappy arrangements. A man may sit on the bottom of the seesaw, or a couple may keep the seesaw moving over time, or each partner may compete with the other for the more helpless, one-down position.

What is important is that being at the bottom of the seesaw relationship is *culturally prescribed* for women. While individual women may defy or even reverse the prescription, it in fact underlies our very definitions of "femininity" and the whole ethos of male dominance. Women are actively taught to cultivate and express all those qualities that men fear in themselves and do not wish to be "weakened" by. And, of course, cultural teachings that discourage us from competing with men or expressing anger at them are paradoxical warnings of how hurtful and destructive the "weaker sex" might be to men if we were simply to be ourselves!

Sure enough, those old dictates to "play dumb," "let the man win," or "pretend he's boss"—are out of vogue. But their message still remains a guiding rule that lurks in the unconscious of countless women: *The weaker sex must protect the stronger sex from recognizing the strength of the weaker sex lest the stronger sex feel weakened by the strength of the weaker sex.* We learn to act weaker to help men feel stronger and to strengthen men by relinquishing our own strength.

Underfunctioning can take any number of forms. It may be as subtle as a wife's turning down a job opportunity or avoiding a new challenge when her husband gives a covert communication that he would prefer things to remain as they are or when she fears he would feel threatened by such a change. A woman may protect her man by confining herself to work that he prefers not to do and by failing to recognize and develop interests and skills in "his" areas. She may, in the process, acquire emotional or physical problems. Underlying her various complaints lurks the unconscious conviction that she must remain in a position of relative weakness for her most important relationship to survive. If the woman is further convinced that she herself cannot survive without the relationship, she will—like Barbara— vent her anger in a manner that only reinforces the old familiar patterns from which her anger stems.

INEFFECTIVE BLAMING VERSUS ASSERTIVE CLAIMING

How does fighting and blaming actually serve to *block* rather than *facilitate* change? Let's analyze Barbara's situation more closely. To begin with, Barbara participated in a dead-end battle about going to the workshop and used her anger energy to try to make her husband see things her way. There are two problems with her efforts to change her husband's mind: First, he has as much right to his opinions and speculations about the workshop as she has to hers. Second, it is hardly likely that she is going to succeed in this venture. She may know from past experience that this particular workshop is just the thing that her husband would say no to. As she said in her phone call, "I'm *sure* the workshop is worth the money, but I couldn't convince him of that. 'No' was his final word."

By engaging in a battle that she could only lose, she failed to exercise the power that she really did have—the power to take charge of her own self. Barbara would have taken a significant step out of her de-selfed position had she clarified her own priorities and taken action on her own behalf. She might have refused to fight entirely and instead said to her husband, "Good or bad, radical or not, the workshop is important to me. If I cancel my registration because you want me to, I will end up feeling angry and resentful. I look forward to the workshop and I plan to go."

What prevented Barbara from moving from ineffective fighting and complaining to clear and assertive claiming? Perhaps she feared paying a very high price for this move. Many of us who fight ineffectively, like those of us who don't fight at all, have an unconscious belief that the other person would have a very hard time if we were clear and strong. *Our anxiety and guilt about the potential loss of a relationship may make it difficult for us to change in the first place—and then to stay on course when our partner reacts strongly to our new and different behavior.*

Making Changes—Taking Chances

What if Barbara did something different and clarified a new position with her husband? What if she approached him at a time when he would be most receptive to hearing her and stated her position firmly and calmly without anger or tears? For instance: "I know that you don't think the workshop is worth the money and I appreciate that this is your opinion. However, I'm a grown woman and I need to make my own decisions. I don't expect you to approve of the workshop or to be happy about my going, but I *do* need to make this decision for myself."

Let us imagine that Barbara could stand firm on the *real* issue here ("I will make my own decisions") and avoid getting sidetracked into arguing other points, such as the value of the workshop or my character and credentials. Let us suppose that without fighting, blaming, accusing, or trying to change her husband's mind, she simply held to her statement of what she wanted to do: "Right or wrong, good or bad, I need to make this choice for myself."

What next? What would happen to this couple if Barbara challenged the status quo by calmly asserting her decision to attend the workshop? What would her husband's next move be? Would he draw the line and say, "If you go, I'll leave you?" Would he say nothing but then hit the bottle, have an affair, or become abusive in some way? Would he respond more mildly and become grouchy or depressed for several days?

Of course, we don't have the slightest idea. We know little about this couple. One thing, however, is certain: Whenever one person makes a move to rebalance the seesaw, there is a countermove by the other party. If Barbara behaved in this new way, her husband would make some "Change back!" maneuver as an attempt to reduce his own anxiety and reinstate the old familiar patterns of fighting. Such a maneuver would occur not because he no longer loved his wife or because he was intimidated by this particular workshop, but because he felt threatened by the new level of assertiveness, separateness, and maturity that Barbara was demonstrating.

Barbara's new position would have implications far beyond the question of her attendance at an anger workshop. It would be a statement that it is her responsibility, not his, to make decisions about what she will and will not do. In calmly and firmly clarifying this important issue in the relationship, she would no longer be the same woman whom he married and with whom he feels comfortable and secure. She, too, would be feeling very anxious and uncertain if she behaved in this new and different way. *There are few things more anxiety-arousing than shifting to a higher level of self-assertion and separateness in an important relationship and maintaining this position despite the countermoves of the other person.*

If Barbara gives up her fantasy that she can change her husband and starts using that same anger energy to clarify her choices and take new actions on her own behalf, she will be less troubled by the "anger problems" that spring from her de-selfed or underfunctioning position: headaches, low self-esteem, and chronic bitterness and dissatisfaction, to name just a few. The price she will pay is that her marriage, at least for a while, will likely be rougher than ever. Underlying issues and conflicts will begin to surface. She may start asking herself some serious questions: "Who is responsible for making decisions about my life?" "How are power and decision-making shared in this relationship?" "What will happen in my marriage if I become stronger and more assertive?" "If my choice is either to sacrifice myself to keep the marriage calm, or to grow and risk losing the relationship, which do I want?"

Perhaps Barbara is not ready to be struggling with such threatening issues at this time. Perhaps she would get very little support in such a venture. Perhaps she believes that any relationship is better than no relationship at all. For all we know, she herself is scared to attend the workshop and is unconsciously inviting her husband to express all the negative feelings for both of them.

It is important to appreciate that there are real dangers here. If Barbara was to stand firm about the workshop, she would inevitably feel an internal pressure to take a stand on other issues as well. Whereas in the past she and her husband may have fit together like two pieces of a puzzle, she would now be in the process of changing her shape. Would he change along with her so that they could continue to fit together, or would he eventually leave her? Would she, while making her own changes, decide that she needed to leave him? At least for now, Barbara has made her choice to protect her husband and continue in the old ways. It is not simply an act of "passive submission"; rather, it may well be an active choice to safeguard the predictable familiarity and security of her most important relationship—her marriage.

PEACE AT ANY PRICE

In a certain way, Barbara is not so "unliberated" as she may seem. She is able to express ideas and opinions that are different from her husband's. She can recognize that what she wants for herself is not the same as what her husband wants for her. She also knows her priorities. She would prefer, at least in this instance, to accommodate to her husband's wishes rather than risk rocking the marital boat.

Many of us make such choices without being consciously aware of what we are doing and why we are doing it. We do not allow our own selves to know that we would like to attend a workshop on anger. We avoid entertaining new ideas and ways of thinking that would lead to overt conflict and disagreement in our relationships with important others. We may not allow ourselves to identify the unfair arrangements in which we participate. We may also cancel our registration to things new and different, but we may be unaware of the sacrifices we make to keep things on an even keel and ensure that peace reigns.

How might such a peace-keeper have handled the

workshop situation? Most likely, she would not have struggled with her partner, because there would have been nothing to fight about. She would not have considered attending an anger workshop in the first place. She would not allow herself to become seriously interested in anything that would threaten another person or disrupt the status quo in an important relationship. If she did allow herself some initial interest in the workshop, she might test out her partner's reaction before she signed up. She might approach him and say, "Listen, I'm thinking about attending this workshop. . . ." And then she would sensitively evaluate his spoken and unspoken response. If she picked up any signals that he felt threatened or was disapproving, she would move in quickly to protect him. She might say to herself, "Well, the workshop probably wouldn't be that good," or, "We don't have the money now," or, "I'm not really in the mood to go, anyway."

In this way, a woman avoids conflict by defining her own wishes and preferences as being the same as what her partner wishes and prefers her to be. She defines her own self as he defines her. She sacrifices her awareness of who she is in her efforts to conform to his wants and expectations. The entire de-selfing process goes on unconsciously so that she may experience herself in perfect harmony with her husband. If she develops emotional or physical problems, she may not associate her dysfunction with the self-sacrifices that she has made in order to protect another person or keep a relationship calm.

In a somewhat less extreme position is the woman who would be able to maintain her interest in the workshop despite the risk of recognizing that she and her partner were not of one mind. She would allow herself to be aware that she is a separate and different person from him, with ideas and preferences no less deserving of respect than his. Nonetheless, she might still find a way to avoid bringing differences between her and her partner into bold relief and incurring his disapproval. She might say to herself, "Well, I do want to go to the workshop, but I can tell there's going to be a big hassle if I push it and it's not worth the fight." *"It's not worth the fight"* is a familiar phrase that protects many of us from confronting the challenge of changing our behavior. As Barbara's situation illustrates, fighting per se is not the issue. What matters is the degree to which we are able to take a clear position in a relationship and behave in ways that are congruent with our stated beliefs.

Women who fall into the peace-maker or "nice lady" category are by no means passive, wishy-washy losers. Quite to the contrary, we have developed an important and complex interpersonal skill that requires a great deal of inner activity and sensitivity. We are good at anticipating other people's reactions, and we are experts at protecting others from uncomfortable feelings. This is a highly developed social skill that is all too frequently absent in men. If only we could take this very same skill and redirect it inward in order to become experts on our own selves.

SEPARATION AND TOGETHERNESS

Making a long-term relationship work is a difficult business because it requires the capacity to strike a balance between individualism (the "I") and togetherness (the "we"). The tugs in both directions are very strong. On the one hand, we want to be separate, independent individuals—self-contained persons in our own right; on the other, we seek a sense of connectedness and intimacy with another person, as well as a sense of belongingness to a family or a group. When a couple gets out of balance in either direction, there is a problem.

What happens if there is not enough "we" in our relationship? The result may be a case of "emotional divorce." Two people can end up isolated and alone in an empty-shell marriage where they do not share personal feelings and experiences. When the "separateness force" is overriding, an "I-don't-need-you" attitude may be expressed by one or both partners—a stance that is a far cry from a truly autonomous position. There may be little fighting in the relationship, but little closeness as well.

What happens if there is not enough "I" in our relationship? Here, we sacrifice our clear and separate identity and our sense of responsibility for, and control over, our own life. When the "togetherness force" is overriding, a lot of energy goes into trying to "be for" the other person, and trying to make the other person think or behave differently. Instead of taking responsibility for our own selves, we tend to feel responsible for the emotional well-being of the other person and hold the other person responsible for ours. When this reversal of individual responsibility is set in motion, each partner may become very emotionally reactive to what the other says and does, and there may be a lot of fighting and blaming, as in Barbara's case.

Another outcome of excessive togetherness is a pseudo-harmonious "we," where there is little overt conflict because a submissive spouse accepts the "reality" of the dominant spouse, or both may behave as if they share a common brain and bloodline. The "urge to merge" may be universal, but when acted out in extreme forms, these "fusion relationships" place us in a terribly vulnerable position. If two people become one, a separation can feel like a psychological or a physical death. We may have nothing—not even a self to fall back on—when an important relationship ends.

We all need to have both an "I" and a "we" that nourish and give meaning to each other. There is no formula for the "right" amount of separateness and togetherness for all couples or even for the same couple over time. Each member of a couple is constantly monitoring the balance of these two forces, automatically and unconsciously making moves to restore more separateness (when anxiety about fusion sets in) or more togetherness (when anxiety about unrelatedness sets in). The balance of these two forces is constantly in motion in every couple. One common "solution" or "division of labor" that couples unconsciously arrange is that the woman will express the wish for "togetherness"; the man, the wish for "separateness." We will be taking a closer look at this dance between the "pursuing female" and the "distancing male" in Chapter 3.

If we are chronically angry or bitter in a particular relationship, that may be a message to clarify and strengthen the "I" a bit more. We must re-examine our own selves with a view toward discovering what we think, feel, and want and what we need to do differently in our lives. The more we carve out a clear and separate "I," the more we can experience and enjoy both intimacy and aloneness. Our intimacy need not be "sameness" or "oneness" or loss of self; our aloneness and separateness need not be distance and isolation.

Why is strengthening the "I" such a difficult task? There are many factors, but if we keep a narrow focus on the here and now, Barbara's situation illustrates how scary it can be to move to a higher level of clarity and assertiveness. Barbara could not give up her old ways and try out some new ones without experiencing an anxiety-arousing feeling of separateness and without making waves in her marriage. Since this is true in all relationships, let's take a closer look.

Clarity and the Fear of Loss

If Barbara had a clearer "I" to begin with, she would not define her problem as: "My husband won't let me go to the workshop." Instead, she might say something like the following to herself: "My problem is this: If I cancel the workshop, I will feel bitter and resentful. If I go to the workshop, my husband will feel bitter and resentful. Which do I choose?" After some thought, she might decide that the workshop was not that important or that the timing just wasn't right for her to make waves in the marriage. Or, she might conclude that the workshop was a non-negotiable issue on which she would not compromise. In this case, she might think about how to present her decision to her husband in a way that would minimize the power struggle. Or, she might simply inform him that she was going. Later, when things were calm, she might initiate a discussion about decision-making in the marriage and explain that while she was interested in his opinions, she was ultimately in charge of making her own decisions.

What stopped Barbara from achieving this kind of clarity? Why would any of us end up as chronic fighters and complainers, rather than identify our problems and choices and clarify our position? No, women do not gain a secret masochistic gratification from being in the victimized, one-down position. Quite to the contrary, the woman who sits at the bottom of a seesaw marriage accumulates a great amount of rage, which is in direct proportion to the degree of her submission and sacrifice.

The dilemma is that we may unconsciously be convinced that our important relationships can survive only if we continue to remain one down. To do better—to become clearer, to act stronger, to be more separate, to take action on our own behalf—may be unconsciously equated with a destructive act that will diminish and threaten our partner, who might then retaliate or leave. Sometimes, to develop a stronger "I" is to come to terms with our deep-seated wish to leave an unsatisfactory marriage, and this possibility may be no less frightening than the fear of being left.

Perhaps Barbara is not ready to face the risk of putting her husband and herself to the test of whether change is possible. She may already be convinced that the relationship cannot tolerate much change. She may be caught between a rock and a hard place: Neither is she ready to say to herself, "I am choosing to stay in this unhappy marriage with a man who is not going to change," nor can she clarify a bottom line and say, "If these things do not change, I will leave." Or perhaps Barbara is not yet ready to face anxiety or the "funny depression" that often hits us when we take a clearer and more separate stance in a meaningful relationship. _Fighting and blaming is sometimes a way both to protest and to protect the status quo when we are not quite ready to make a move in one direction or another._

COUNTERMOVES AND "CHANGE BACK!" REACTIONS

I do not wish to convey the bleak impression that we must stay put on the bottom of the seesaw lest our partner, as well as our relationship, come tumbling down. In some cases, this may happen as a consequence of our change and growth. But more frequently, and depending on how we proceed, the other person will grow along with us, and our emotional ties will ultimately be strengthened. We can learn to strengthen our own selves in a way that will maximize the chances that we will enhance rather than threaten our relationships. Making a change, however, never occurs easily and smoothly.

We meet with a countermove or "Change back!" reaction from the other person whenever we begin to give up the old ways of silence, vagueness, or ineffective fighting and begin to make clear statements about the needs, wants, beliefs, and priorities of the self. In fact, Murray Bowen, the originator of Bowen Family Systems Theory, emphasizes the fact that in *all* families there is a powerful opposition to one member defining a more independent self. According to Bowen, the opposition invariably goes in successive steps:

1. "You are wrong," with volumes of reasons to support this.
2. "Change back and we will accept you again."
3. "If you don't change back, these are the consequences," which are then listed.

What are some common countermoves? We may be accused of coldness, disloyalty, selfishness, or disregard for others. ("How could you upset your mother by saying that to her!") We may receive verbal or nonverbal threats that the other person will withdraw or terminate the relationship. ("We can't be close if you feel that way." "How can we have a relationship if you really mean that?") Countermoves take any number of forms. For example, a person may have an asthma attack or even a stroke.

Countermoves are the other person's unconscious attempt to restore a relationship to its prior balance or equilibrium, when anxiety about separateness and change gets too high. Other people do not make countermoves simply because they are dominating, controlling, or chauvinistic. They may or may not be these things, but that is almost beside the point. Countermoves are an expression of anxiety, as well as of closeness and attachment.

Our job is to keep clear about our own position in the face of a countermove—not to prevent it from happening or to tell the other person that he or she should not be reacting that way. Most of us want the impossible. We want to control not only our own decisions and choices but also the other person's *reactions* to them. We not only want to make a change; we want the other person to *like* the change that we make. We want to move ahead to a higher level of assertiveness and clarity and then receive praise and reinforcement from those very people who have chosen us for our old familiar ways.

Countermoves aside, our *own* resistance to change is just as formidable a force. Barbara's position in her marriage, for example, may have roots in patterns that go back for many generations. Barbara's mother and other women relatives who came before her may have assumed a de-selfed position in marriage, or may have paired up with de-selfed husbands. There may not be a tradition in Barbara's family for marriages in which *both* partners can be clear and competent in making decisions about their own lives and negotiating differences. All of us are deeply affected by the patterns and traditions of past generations even if—and especially if—we are not consciously aware of them. Like many women, Barbara may feel guilty if she strives to have for herself what her own mother could not. Deep in her unconscious mind, Barbara may view her attempt at self-assertion as an act of disloyalty—a betrayal not only of her husband but also of generations of women in her family. If this is the case, she will unconsciously resist the changes that she seeks.

To complicate matters further, unresolved issues from our past inevitably surface in our current relationships. If Barbara is stuck in a pattern of chronic marital fighting and blaming, that may be a sign that she has not negotiated her separateness and independence within her first family and that she needs to do some work here (see Chapter 4). How well is Barbara able to take a firm position on important issues with members of her first family? Is she able to make clear and direct statements of her own thoughts and feelings? Is she able to be who she is and not what other family members want or expect her to be—and allow others to do the same? If Barbara is having difficulty staying in emotional contact with living members of her first family and defining a clear and separate "I" within this context, she may have difficulty doing so in her marriage. As a psychotherapist I often help women to clarify and to change their relationships with siblings, parents, and grandparents so that underground family conflicts and patterns will not be replayed—nor buried anger and anxieties pop up—in another close relationship, making for a painful degree of reactivity to others.

WHERE ARE WE?

Barbara's telephone call provided us with an excellent example of ineffective fighting that ensures non-change, because she did two things that we all do when we are stuck and spinning our wheels: First, she fought about a false issue.

Second, she put her energy into trying to change the other person.

Pseudo Issues

Barbara and her husband probably put a great deal of energy into fighting about the value of my workshop, which is, like most things in life, a matter of personal opinion. More to the point, it's a pseudo issue. It has nothing to do with Barbara's real problem, which concerns her struggle between her wish to make responsible decisions for her own life and her wish to preserve togetherness in her marriage and protect the status quo.

All couples fight over pseudo issues some of the time, and often with great intensity. I will never forget the very first couple I saw in marital therapy. There in my office they sat, quarreling bitterly over whether they would eat their dinner that evening at McDonald's or Long John Silver's. Each of these intelligent people put forth the most compelling arguments regarding the relative merits of hamburger or fish, and neither would give an inch. Being new at marital therapy, I was not quite certain how to be helpful to this couple, but I did know one thing for sure: The impassioned argument I was witnessing between two people who were obviously in a great deal of pain had nothing to do with the respective value of burgers and fish.

Identifying the *real* issues is no easy matter. It is particularly difficult among family members, because when two adults have a conflict, they often bring in a third party (perhaps a child or an in-law) to form a triangle, which then makes it even harder for the two people involved to identify and work out their problems. For example:

A wife says to her husband, "I am terribly angry about the way you ignore our son. I feel like he's growing up without a father." The real issue not addressed is: "I feel ignored and I am angry that you do not spend more time with me."

A husband says to his wife, who is considering a new job, "The children need you at home. I support your working, but I do not like to see the kids and the household neglected." The real issue not addressed is: "I am scared and worried about your making this change. I am not sure how your career will affect our relationship, and your enthusiasm about this new work is putting me in touch with my dissatisfaction with my own job."

A wife says to her husband, "Your mother is driving me crazy. She's intrusive and controlling and she treats you like you're her husband and little boy all wrapped up in one." The real issue not addressed is: "I wish you could be more assertive with your mother and set some limits. Sometimes I wonder whether your primary commitment is to me or to her."

When we learn about triangles (Chapter 8), we will see that it is difficult to sort out not only *what* we are angry about but also *whom* we are angry at.

Trying to Change Him

Barbara, like most of us, was putting her "anger energy" into trying to change the other person. She was trying to change her husband's thoughts and feelings about the workshop and his reactions to her going. She wanted him to approve of the workshop and she wanted him to *want* her to go. In short, she wanted him to think and feel about the workshop as she did. Of course, most of us secretly believe that we have the corner on the "truth" and that this would be a much better world if everyone else believed and reacted exactly as we do. But one of the hallmarks of emotional maturity is to recognize the validity of multiple realities and to understand that people think, feel, and react differently. Often we behave as if "closeness" means "sameness." Married couples and family members are especially prone to behave as if there is one "reality" that should be agreed upon by all.

It is extremely difficult to learn, with our hearts as well as our heads, that we have a right to everything we think and feel—and so does everyone else. It *is* our job to state our thoughts and feelings clearly and to make responsible decisions that are congruent with our values and beliefs. It is *not* our job to make another person think and feel the way we do or the way we want them to. If we try, we can end up in a relationship in which a lot of personal pain and emotional intensity are being expended and nothing is changing.

There is nothing wrong with *wanting* to change someone else. The problem is that it usually doesn't work. No matter how skilled we become in dealing with our anger, we cannot ensure that another person will do what we want him or her to or see things our way, nor are we guaranteed that justice will prevail. We are able to move away from ineffective fighting only when we give up the fantasy that we can change or control another person. It is only then that we can reclaim the power that is truly ours—the power to change our own selves and take a new and different action on our own behalf.

In the chapters that follow, we will learn how to put the lessons from Barbara's phone call into practice. What are these seemingly simple lessons?

First, "letting it all hang out" may not be helpful, because venting anger may protect rather than challenge the old rules and patterns in a relationship. Second, the only person we can change and control is our own self. Third, changing our own self can feel so threatening and difficult that it is often easier to continue an old pattern of silent withdrawal or ineffective fighting and blaming. And, finally, de-selfing is at the heart of our most serious anger problems.

3

CIRCULAR DANCES
IN COUPLES
When Getting Angry
Is Getting Nowhere

Six months after the birth of my first son, I was vacationing
with my family in Berkeley, California. Browsing through a
secondhand bookstore, I came upon a volume by a foremost
expert in child development. My heart sank slightly as I
noted that my baby was not doing the things that the book
said were appropriate for his age. "My God," I thought to
myself, "my child is slow!" I flashed back on the complications
that had characterized my pregnancy, and I froze. Was
something wrong with my baby?

When I saw my husband, Steve, later in the day, I
anxiously told him my fears. He responded with uncharacteristic insensitivity. "Forget it," he said matter-of-factly. "Babies develop at different rates. He's fine." His response (which
I heard as an attempt to silence me) only upset me further. I
reacted by trying to prove my point. I told him in detail what
the book said, and I reminded him of the problems I had
experienced throughout the pregnancy. He accused me of
exaggerating the problem and of worrying excessively. *Nothing* was wrong. I accused him of denying and minimizing

the problem. Something *might* be wrong. He reminded me coldly that my mother was a "worrier" and that, clearly, I was following in her footsteps. I reminded him angrily that worrying was not permitted in *his* family, since problems were not to be noticed. And then followed more of the same.

We repeated this *same* fight, in its *same* form, countless times over the next six months as our son continued even more conspicuously *not* to do what the book said he should be doing. The psychologist who tested him at nine months (at my initiation) said that he was, in fact, quite slow in certain areas but that it was too early to know what this meant. She suggested that we wait a while and then consult with a pediatric neurologist if we were still concerned.

Steve and I became even more rigidly polarized in our fights, and we fought with increasing frequency. Like robots, we took the same repetitive positions, and the sequence unfolded as neatly as clockwork: The more I expressed worry and concern, the more Steve distanced and minimized; the more he distanced and minimized, the more I exaggerated my position. This sequence would escalate until it finally became intolerable, at which point each of us would angrily point the finger at the other for "starting it."

We were stuck. Our years of psychological training and intellectual sophistication went down the drain. It was clear enough that what each of us was doing only provoked a more vehement stance in the other. Yet, somehow, neither Steve nor I was able to do something different ourselves.

"Your baby is fine," a top pediatric neurologist in Kansas City reported blandly. Our son was almost a year old. "He has an atypical developmental pattern. There are certain babies who don't do much of anything until they walk." Sure enough, our son began to walk (right on schedule, no less) without having crawled, scooted, or in any way moved about preceding this. And so ended our chronic repetitive fights.

Later, we were able to recognize the unconscious benefits we got by maintaining these fights. Fighting with each other helped both of us to worry a little less about our son, and deflected our attention from other concerns we had about becoming new parents. But what was most impressive at the time was how irrevocably stuck we were. We both behaved as if there was only one "right" way to respond to a stressful situation in the family, and we engaged in a dance in which we were trying to get the *other* person to change steps while we would not change our own. The outcome was that nothing changed at all.

GETTING STUCK—GETTING UNSTUCK

How do couples get stuck? The inability to express anger is not always at the heart of the problem. Many women, like myself, get angry with ease and have no difficulty showing it. Instead, the problem is that getting angry is getting nowhere, or even making things worse.

If what we are doing with our anger is not achieving the desired result, it would seem logical to try something different. In my case, I could have changed my behavior with Steve in a number of ways. Surely, it was clear to me that my anxious expressions of worry only provoked his denial, which then provoked more worry on my part. For example, I might have taken my worry to a good friend for several weeks and stopped expressing it to Steve. Perhaps then Steve would have had the opportunity to experience his own worry. Or, I might have approached Steve at a time when we were close, and shared with him that I was worrying a lot about our baby and that I hoped for his help and support as I struggled with this. Such an approach would have been quite different from my usual behavior, which involved speaking out at the very height of my anxiety and then implying that Steve was at fault for not reacting the same way as I. Steve, too, might easily have broken the pattern of our fights by doing something different himself. For example, *he* might have initiated a talk in which he expressed concern for our son.

We all recognize intellectually that repeating our ineffective efforts achieves nothing and can even make things worse. Yet, oddly enough, most of us continue to do *more of the same*, especially under stress. For example, a wife who lectures her husband about his failure to stay on his diet increases the intensity or frequency of her lectures when he overeats. A woman whose lover becomes cooler when she angrily presses him to express feelings presses on even harder, her problem being not that she is unable to get angry but that she's doing something with her anger that isn't working and yet keeps doing it.

Even rats in a maze learn to vary their behavior if they keep hitting a dead end. Why in the world, then, do we behave less intelligently than laboratory animals? The answer, by now, may be obvious. Repeating the same old fights protects us from the anxieties we are bound to experience when we make a change. Ineffective fighting allows us to stop the clock when our efforts to achieve greater clarity become too threatening. Sometimes staying stuck is what we need to do until the time comes when we are confident that it is safe to get unstuck.

Sometimes, however, even when we *are* ready to risk

change, we still keep participating in the same old familiar fights that go nowhere. Human nature is such that when we are angry, we tend to become so emotionally reactive to what the other person is doing to us that we lose our ability to observe our own part in the interaction. Self-observation is not at all the same as self-blame, at which some women are experts. Rather, self-observation is the process of seeing the interaction of ourselves and others, and recognizing that the ways other people behave with us has something to do with the way we behave with them. We cannot *make* another person be different, but when we do something different ourselves, the old dance can no longer continue as usual.

The story of Sandra and Larry, a couple who sought my help, is a story about getting unstuck. While the *content* of their struggles may or may not hit home, the *form* of the dance they do together is almost universal. For this couple, like many, was caught in a circular dance in which the behavior of each served to maintain and provoke that of the other. Once we are part of an established twosome—married or unmarried, lesbian or straight—we may easily become caught in such a dance. When this happens, the more each person tries to change things, the more things stay the same.

SANDRA AND LARRY

"Well, how do each of you see the problem in your marriage?" I inquired. It was my first meeting with Sandra and Larry, who had requested marital therapy at Sandra's initiative. My eyes fell first on Larry and then on Sandra, who quickly picked up the invitation to speak. She turned her body in my direction and cupped her hands against her face. Like blinders, they blocked Larry from her view.

With unveiled anger in her voice, Sandra listed her complaints. It was evident that she had told her story before. It was also evident that she thought the "problem" was her husband.

"First of all, he's a workaholic," she began. "He neglects the kids and me. I don't even think he knows how to relate to us anymore. He's a stranger in his own family." Sandra paused for a moment, drew a deep breath, and continued: "He acts like he expects me to run the house and deal with the kids all by myself, and then when something goes wrong, he tells me I'm crazy to be reacting so emotionally. He's not available and he never expresses his feelings about things that should worry him."

"When Larry comes home, and you're upset about something at home, how do you ask for his support and help?" I asked.

"I tell him that I'm really upset, that I'm worried about our money situation, and that Jeff is sick, and that I had to miss my class, and that I'm going nuts with the baby today. But he just looks at me and criticizes me that the dinner isn't ready, or tells me that I'm overreacting. He always says, 'Why do you get so damn emotional about everything?' He makes me want to scream!"

Sandra fell silent and Larry said nothing. After several minutes, Sandra continued, her anger now laced with tears: "I'm tired of being at the bottom of his list of priorities. He hardly ever takes the initiative to relate to me and he neglects the kids, too. And then, when he *does* decide that he wants to be a father, he just takes over like he's the only one in charge."

"For example?" I asked.

"For example, he goes out and buys Lori, our oldest

daughter, this expensive dressing table that she's had her
eye on, and he doesn't even consult me! He just tells me after
the fact!" Sandra is now glaring at Larry, who refuses to
meet her eye.

"When Larry does something that you disapprove of,
like the dressing-table incident, how do you let him know?"

"It's impossible!" Sandra said emphatically. "It's simply
impossible!"

"*What* is impossible?" I persisted.

"Talking to him! Confronting him! He doesn't talk about
feelings. He doesn't know how to discuss things. He just
doesn't respond. He clams up and wants to be left alone. He
doesn't even know how to fight. Either he talks in this
superlogical manner, or he refuses to talk at all. He'd rather
read a book or turn on the television."

"Okay," I said, "I think I understand how you see the
problem." It was Larry's turn now: "How do you define the
problem in your marriage, Larry?"

Larry proceeded to speak in a controlled and deliberate
voice that almost masked the fact that he was as angry as
his wife: "Sandra isn't supportive enough, she doesn't give
enough, and she's always on my back. I think that's the main
problem." Larry fell silent, as if he was finished for the day.

"In what ways does Sandra fail to support you or give
to you? Can you share a specific example?"

"Well, it's hard to say. She cuts me down a lot, for one
thing. Or, I walk in the door at six o'clock, and I'm tired and
wanting some peace and quiet, and she just rattles on about
the kids' problems or her problems, or she just complains
about one thing or another. Or, if I sit down to relax for five
minutes, she's on my back to discuss some earthshaking
matter—like the garbage disposal is broken." Larry was

angry, but he managed to sound as if he was discussing the Dow-Jones average.

"Are you saying that you need some space?" I asked.

"Not exactly," replied Larry. "I'm saying that Sandra is very overreactive. She's very overemotional. She creates problems where they don't even exist. Everything is a major case. And, yes, I suppose I am saying that I need more space."

"What about the kids? Do you—" I had not finished my question when Larry interrupted:

"Sandra is a very overinvolved mother," he explained carefully, as if he were describing a patient at a clinical conference. "She worries excessively about the children. She inherited it from her mother. And, if you could meet her mother, you would understand."

"Do you worry about the kids?" I inquired.

"Only when there's something to worry about. For Sandra, it seems to be a full-time job."

Although one would not have guessed it from this first session, Sandra and Larry were deeply committed to each other. At our initial meeting, however, they appeared to share only one thing in common—blaming. Like many couples, each spouse saw the locus of his or her marital difficulties as existing entirely within the other person, and each had the same unstated goal for marital therapy—that the *other* would be "fixed up" and "straightened out."

Let's take a closer look at the details of Sandra and Larry's story, for there is much to be learned. Though couples differ markedly in how they present themselves, the ways in which they get stuck are very much the same.

"He Just Doesn't Respond!"
"She's Very Overemotional!"

Sound familiar? Sandra and Larry's central complaints about each other will ring a bell for many couples. His unfeelingness, unavailability, and distance is a major source of her anger: "My husband withdraws from confrontation and cannot share his real feelings." "My husband is like a machine." "My husband refuses to talk about things." "My husband is more invested in his work than in his family." And it is no coincidence that men have a reciprocal complaint: "My wife is much too reactive." "She gets irrational much too easily." "I wish that she would back off and stop nagging and bitching." "My wife wants to talk everything to death."

As typically happens, the very qualities that each partner complains of in the other are those that attracted them to each other to begin with. Sandra, for example, had been drawn to Larry's orderly, even-keel temperament, just as he had admired her capacity to be emotional and spontaneous. Her reactive, feeling-oriented approach to the world balanced his distant, logical reserve—and vice versa. Opposites attract—right?

Opposites do attract, but they do not always live happily ever after. On the one hand, it is reassuring to live with someone who will express parts of one's own self that one is afraid to acknowledge; yet, the arrangement has its inevitable costs: The woman who is expressing feelings not only for herself but also for her husband will indeed end up behaving "hysterically" and "irrationally." The man who relies on his wife to do the "feeling work" for him will increasingly lose touch with this important part of himself, and when the time comes that he needs to draw upon his emotional resources, he may find that nobody's at home.

In the majority of couples, men sit on the bottom of the seesaw when it comes to emotional competence. We all know about the man who can tie good knots on packages and fix things that break, yet fails to notice that his wife is depressed. He may have little emotional relatedness to his own family and lack even one close friend with whom honest self-disclosure takes place. This is the "masculinity" that our society breeds—the male who feels at home in the world of things and abstract ideas but who has little empathic connection to others, little attunement to his own internal world, and little willingness or capacity to "hang in" when a relationship becomes conflicted and stressful. In the traditional division of labor, men are encouraged to develop one kind of intelligence, but they fall short of another that is equally important. The majority *underfunction* in the realm of emotional competence, and their underfunctioning is closely related to women's *overfunctioning* in this area. It is not by accident that the "hysterical," overemotional female ends up under the same roof as the unemotional, distant male.

The marital seesaw is hard to balance. When couples do try to balance it, especially under stress, their solutions often exacerbate the problem. The emotional, feeling-oriented wife who gets on her husband's back to open up and express feelings will find that he becomes cooler and even less available. The cool, intellectual husband who tries calmly to use logic to quiet his overemotional wife will find that she becomes even more agitated. True to stereotype, each partner continues to do the *same old thing* while trying to change the other. The solution for righting the balance *becomes* the problem.

DOING THE "FEELING WORK" FOR LARRY

Sandra had long been furious at Larry's lack of reactivity without realizing her own part in the circular dance. She failed to recognize that she was so skilled and comfortable in expressing feelings that she was doing the job for the two of them, thus protecting her husband from feeling what he would otherwise feel. Doing the "feeling work," like cleaning up, has long been defined as "woman's work," and lots of women are good at it. As with cleaning up, men will not begin to do their share until women no longer do it for them.

Although it was not her conscious intent, Sandra helped Larry to maintain his underemotional stance by expressing more than her share of emotionality. The unconscious contract for this couple was that Sandra would be the emotional reactor and Larry the rational planner. And so, Sandra reacted *for* Larry. She did so in response not only to family stresses that concerned them both but also to problems that were really Larry's to struggle with. Here are two examples of how Sandra protected Larry by doing the feeling work for him:

An Injustice on the Job

One evening when Larry returned from work, he told Sandra that a co-worker had gotten credit for an idea that was originally his. As he began to outline the details of the incident, Sandra became upset and expressed her strong anger at the injustice. As her emotional involvement in the incident increased, she noticed that Larry was becoming cooler and more removed. "Aren't you upset about this?" she demanded. "It's your life, you know! Don't you have any feelings about it?"

Of course Larry had feelings about it. It was his career and the injustice had been done him. However, his style of reacting, as well as his tempo and timing, was very different from his wife's. Also, Larry was using Sandra to react *for* him. Her quick outburst actually took him off the hook. He did not have to feel upset about the incident because she was doing all the work. The more emotion Sandra displayed, the less Larry felt within himself.

Sandra was consciously angry and frustrated at Larry's apparent lack of feelings about the incident, yet she was unconsciously helping him to maintain his strong, cool, masculine position. By criticizing him for not showing feelings and demonstrating the appropriate degree of distress, she was applying a solution that only reinforced the very problem she complained of. Sandra could not *make* Larry react differently. However, she could do something different herself. When Sandra stopped doing the feeling work for Larry, the circular dance was broken.

It was not easy for Sandra to change her behavior, but eventually she did make an important shift: Sometime later, when Larry shared a crisis at work, Sandra listened calmly and quietly. She did not express feelings that appropriately belonged to Larry, nor did she offer solutions to a problem that was not hers. Given sufficient time and space around him, Larry did, indeed, begin to react to his own problem and struggle with his own dilemma. In fact, he became depressed. But, while this was the very reaction Sandra had overtly sought and wished for ("That cool bastard doesn't react to anything!"), she was uncomfortable seeing her husband vulnerable and struggling. She realized, to her surprise, that part of her wanted Larry to maintain the role of the cool, strong, unruffled partner.

A Problem with Larry's Parents

Sandra also protected Larry from recognizing his anger at his own parents. She did this by criticizing them and fuming at them *for* him. Larry, then, was left with the simpler job of coming to their defense.

This pattern began at the time of the birth of their first child. Larry's parents, who were quite wealthy, were spending the year in Paris and did not acknowledge their new granddaughter with enthusiasm or show interest in seeing her. Sandra reacted with outrage, declaring to Larry that they were cold and selfish people who thought only of themselves. Years later she still spoke heatedly about their neglectful attitude, although always to Larry and never to his parents.

What did Larry do? He made excuses for his parents and found logical reasons for their behavior, which only made Sandra angrier. It was another circular dance in which the behavior of each provoked the other into doing more of the same. The more Sandra criticized her in-laws to Larry, the more Larry came to their defense; the more Larry came to their defense, the more openly critical Sandra became.

Deep down, of course, Larry was considerably more affected than Sandra by his parents' behavior. They were, after all, his parents, and he was their son. But because of Sandra's readiness to do the feeling work for him, Larry was in touch only with his loyalty to his parents who were under his wife's attack.

Sandra's focus on Larry's behavior with *his* parents, as opposed to her own relationship with *her* in-laws, complicated the problem and the solution. In fact, Sandra's focus on her husband obscured her own need to change matters.

Larry's parents, who traveled a great deal, visited once a year. These visits were initiated by Larry's father, who would write a letter informing the couple when they would arrive and for how long they would stay. Being told rather than asked annoyed Sandra no end. She then put pressure on Larry to confront his parents regarding this matter and he would refuse. In the face of Sandra's anger and criticisms, Larry predictably sided with them, putting forth logical arguments as to why his parents needed to schedule visits as they did.

Sandra felt helpless, and for good reason: First, she was trying to make Larry do something and it wasn't working. Second, she was doing the feeling work for him. Down the road a bit, Sandra changed both of these patterns.

At some point Sandra recognized that if the behavior of Larry's parents upset her, it was her job to deal with this herself. So she did. In a letter that was neither attacking nor blaming, Sandra explained to her in-laws that it was important to her to be consulted in arranging a mutually agreeable time for their visits. She stated her position warmly but with clarity and directness, and she did not back down in the face of their initial defensiveness. Much to her surprise, her long-pent-up anger at her in-laws began to dissipate as she became more confident that she could speak effectively to issues that were not to her liking. Also to her surprise, Larry's parents, in the end, responded warmly and affirmatively, thanking Sandra for her straightforwardness. This was the first step in Sandra's taking care of her own business with her in-laws, and, in the process, opening up a more direct person-to-person relationship with each of them.

Larry, threatened by the new assertiveness that his wife was expressing, initially protested the very idea that she would write such a letter. In his typical style, he presented her with a dozen intellectual arguments to back his disapproval. Sandra, however, was clear in her resolve to change things and resisted fighting back, since her experience had taught her that such arguments led nowhere. Instead, she explained to Larry that although she appreciated his point of view, she needed to make her own decisions about how, when, and if she would deal with issues that were important to her.

When Larry observed that Sandra was continuing to address issues directly with his parents without criticizing or attacking them, a predictable next step occurred: His own unresolved issues with his mother and father surfaced full force. Sandra was no longer complaining to Larry about his parents but managing her own business with them. In response to this, Larry began to feel an internal pressure to take care of his own.

When a woman vents her anger ineffectively (like Sandra complaining to Larry about his parents, which surely wasn't going to change anything), or expresses it in an overemotional style, she does *not* threaten her man. If anything, she helps him to maintain his masculine cool, while she herself is perceived as infantile or irrational. When a woman clarifies the issues and uses her anger to move toward something new and different, then change occurs. If she stops *overfunctioning* for others and starts acting for herself, her *underfunctioning* man is likely to acknowledge and deal with his own anxieties.

THE BLAMING GAME

Sandra and Larry had expended enormous amounts of energy blaming each other for their endless fights. Like many of us, their method of attributing blame was to look for the one who started it. The search for a beginning of a sequence is a common blaming game in couples.

Consider, for example, the interaction between a nagging wife and a distant, withdrawing husband. The more he withdraws, the more she nags, and the more she nags, the more he withdraws, and so on. . . . So, who is to blame?

"I know!" says one observer of this sequence. "She is to blame. *First* she nags him and gets on his case for all kinds of things, and *then* the poor guy withdraws."

"No," says a second observer, "you have it all wrong. He is! *First* he buries himself in his work and ignores his family, and *then* his wife goes after him."

This is the who-started-it game—the search for a beginning of a sequence, where the aim is to proclaim which person is to blame for the behavior of both. But we know that this interaction is really a circular dance in which the behavior of one partner maintains and provokes the behavior of the other. The circular dance has no beginning and no end. In the final analysis, it matters little who started it. The question of greater significance is: "How do we break out of it?"

A good way to make this break is to recognize the part we play in maintaining and provoking the other person's behavior. Even if we are convinced that the other person is ninety-seven percent to blame, we are still in control of changing our own three percent. So the central question becomes: "How can I change *my* steps in the circular dance?" This is not to say that we don't have good reason to be furious with the other person. Nor is it to say that our current sex roles and gender arrangements, which breed these sorts of dances, are not at fault—they are. Rather, it is simply to say that we don't have the power to change another person

who does not want to change, and our atte[mpts]
may actually *protect* him or her from chan[ge. A]
paradox of the circular dances in which we all pa[rt...]

EMOTIONAL PURSUER—EMOTIONAL DISTANCER
A VERY OLD DANCE

Emotional pursuers are persons who reduce their anxiety by
sharing feelings and seeking close emotional contact. Emotional distancers are persons who reduce their anxiety by
intellectualizing and withdrawing. As with Sandra and Larry,
it is most often the woman who is the emotional pursuer
and the man who is the emotional distancer.

When the waters are calm, the pursuer and the distancer
may seem like the perfect complementary couple. She is
spontaneous, lively, and emotionally responsive. He is re-
served, calm, and logical. When the waters are rough, however, each exaggerates his or her own style, and that's where
the trouble begins.

What happens when the inevitable stresses of life hit
this couple? It may be an illness, a child in difficulty, a
financial worry, or a possible career move. No matter what
the content of the problem, these two styles of responding
suddenly seem at odds. She reacts quickly, seeking direct
contact and refuge in togetherness. She shares her feelings
and wants him to do the same. He reacts very logically and
rationally in a manner that is not acceptable to her. So, she
pursues harder, wanting to know more of what he is thinking
and feeling, and he distances further. The more he distances,
the more she pursues, and the more she pursues, the more
he distances. She accuses him of being cold, unresponsive,
and inhuman. He accuses her of being pushy, hysterical, and
controlling.

What is the common outcome of this classic scenario? After this escalating dance of pursuit and withdrawal proceeds for some time, the woman goes into what therapists call "reactive distance." Feeling rejected and fed up, she at last proceeds to go about her own business. The man now has even more space than he is comfortable with, and in time he moves closer to her in the hope of making contact. But it's too late. "Where were you when I needed you!" she says angrily. At this point, distancer and pursuer might even reverse their roles for a while.

Emotional pursuers protect emotional distancers. By doing the work of expressing the neediness, clingingness, and wish for closeness for both partners, pursuers make it possible for distancers to avoid confronting their own dependency wishes and insecurities. As long as one person is pursuing, the other has the luxury of experiencing a cool independence and a need for space. It is hardly surprising, considering her upbringing, that the woman is usually, though by no means always, the pursuer. It is another example of doing the feeling work for men. When a pursuer learns to back off and put her energies into her own life—especially if she can do this with dignity and *without hostility*—the distancer is more likely to recognize his own needs for contact and closeness ... and begin to pursue. But beware, this is no easy task. Most women who are emotional pursuers go off into a cold or angry "reactive distance," which only temporarily reverses the pursuit cycle or has little effect at all.

BREAKING THE PURSUIT CYCLE

Sandra and Larry were caught in an escalating cycle of pursuit and distance for many years prior to their seeking help. Since the birth of their first child, Larry was decreasing his emotional involvement with Sandra as he increased the energy he put into work and hobbies. Sandra alternated between active pursuit, angry criticism, and a cold, bitter withdrawal. Sadly, but predictably, their relationship had gone from bad to worse.

On one particular Friday night, almost a year following our first meeting, Sandra broke the pursuit cycle. It was her increased sense of personal responsibility to provide for her own needs, as well as her growing awareness that she could not change her husband, that allowed her to do something new and different. And something new and different is exactly what Sandra did.

This Friday evening began like all others. The children were in bed, and Larry was shuffling through his briefcase about to pull out a couple hours' work. Sandra came and sat down next to him on the couch. Larry bristled, expecting the usual attack, but it did not come. Instead, Sandra began to speak warmly and with assurance:

"Larry, I feel like I owe you an apology. I've been on your back for a long time. I realize that I have been wanting you to provide me with something that really _I_ need to provide for myself. Perhaps part of the problem is that you have family and work and I have only you and the kids. It's my problem and I recognize that I need to do something about it."

"Oh," muttered Larry, with a somewhat unsettled look on his face. He seemed at an uncharacteristic loss for words. "Well, that's nice. . . ."

The very next night, Sandra asked Larry if he would mind putting the children to bed himself on Tuesday and Friday because she was planning to go out. Larry protested that he had too much work. Instead of arguing, Sandra called the sitter to come in and help on those evenings. On Tuesday night Sandra joined a yoga class that met weekly. On Friday night she went to the movies with a friend and then out for a glass of wine. She did not pursue Larry in any way, nor did she distance from him or withdraw coldly. If anything, she was warmer to him than usual, although clearly directing much of her energy toward her own interests and scheduling.

After three weeks of this, Larry, who had wanted nothing more than to be left alone, began to get nervous. Much to his surprise, he became quite uncomfortable when his wife's bleep was off his radar screen. At first, he tried to provoke her into fighting by attempting to control what she could or could not do with her evenings. Without retaliating, Sandra explained to Larry that she was a social person with social needs and that she was no longer able to neglect this important part of her life. Her warm firmness on this issue communicated clearly to Larry that she was acting *for herself* and not *against him*.

Next, Larry started to pursue her. Instead of bringing his work home, he suggested they use the sitter to go out together—something they almost never did on a week night. As Larry increasingly began to experience and express his own dependency and insecurity, a funny thing happened: Sandra, for the first time, got in touch with her own wish to be left alone. For a while, they simply reversed their roles as pursuer and distancer until, finally, they got things in balance. And when that occurred, Sandra and Larry were able to recognize that each of them harbored strong dependency wishes, as well as a wish to flee when things became "too close."

Why was it Sandra who finally took the initiative in breaking the circular dance? Sandra was in greater emotional pain than Larry, and her role as the pursuer in the relationship placed her in a more emotionally vulnerable position. When she became convinced that her old ways simply were not working for her, she found the motivation to move differently. Why did *she* have to take the responsibility to make the change? Simply because no one else was going to do it for her.

Breaking the pursuit cycle did not in itself lead to emotional closeness for Sandra and Larry; there were important barriers to intimacy that the two of them were left to struggle with. However, Sandra and Larry could work more successfully on their relationship once they recognized that they shared a common problem: Both of them wished for closeness and also feared it. Before Sandra broke the pursuit cycle, Larry had the false but comforting fantasy that all of the neediness and wish for closeness was in Sandra. Likewise, Sandra imagined that all of the avoidance of and flight from intimacy was in Larry.

When a pursuer stops pursuing and begins to put her energy back into her own life—without distancing or expressing anger at the other person—the circular dance has been broken. Because this may smack of the old "hard-to-get" tactics that women have been taught to play, it may sound inauthentic or manipulative. But continuing the old dance of pursuit or cold withdrawal is *not* more honest. In fact, it only leaves the woman feeling the neediness and dependency for two people, while her partner can disown these same qualities within himself. Our experience of a relationship becomes more "true" and balanced as the pursuer can allow herself to acknowledge and express more of her own wish for independence and space, and, in turn, the distancer can begin to acknowledge more of his dependency and wish for closeness.

OVERINVOLVED MOTHER—UNDERINVOLVED
FATHER: THE LAST DANCE

"Sandra is a very overinvolved mother. She inherited it from her mother." These were Larry's words about Sandra's mothering during our first meeting. And it was true. Sandra did worry excessively about the children, as her own mother had worried about her. She became upset when her children were upset, and she had difficulty allowing them to handle their own disappointments and deal with their own sadness and anger. She was quick to spot potential "problems" in her children in a way that actually invited them to give her something to worry about. Larry was correct that Sandra was an overinvolved mother. However, he was unaware of his part in provoking and maintaining that circular dance.

Larry's singular pursuit of career goals had left him estranged from his wife and children and lacking in parenting skills. As Sandra moved in even closer to fill the empty space left by Larry, Larry felt more shut out and withdrew further. Whenever his anger about being on the periphery caught up with him, he moved in with a bang! As Sandra described in our initial meeting, he then took over in a unilateral way, as if he was the only one in charge. Underlying his sporadic displays of paternal dominance was his sadness and anger about his actual position as "odd man out" in the family. And so, Sandra and Larry were caught in another dance in which the behavior of each spouse provokes and reinforces the behavior of the other. Larry's underinvolvement provoked Sandra's overinvolvement, which provoked Larry's underinvolvement . . . Thus, the vicious cycle continued, punctuated by Larry's occasional displays of dominance, following which their life returned to its usual pattern.

This dance was very difficult to disrupt, because the entire family was working overtime to keep it going: On the one hand, Sandra and Larry each demanded that the other change. Larry criticized Sandra's overinvolvement with the children as harshly as she criticized his token fathering. Yet, each of them also wanted to keep the old dance going. "Please change!" and "Change back!" was the double message they gave each other. Like most couples, each partner wished for the other's change and growth, yet feared and resisted it.

Sandra, for example, complained incessantly about Larry's underinvolvement with the children. Yet, when he did make a tentative move closer to the family, she would correct some detail of his parenting, criticize some aspect of his behavior, or advise him on how to better interact with the children. It was extremely difficult for her to simply stay out and allow him to relate to the children in his own way. Sandra wanted Larry to become more involved, but she also wanted to maintain her special role as the more dominant and influential parent. If she relinquished that special status, her feelings of uselessness threatened to become intolerably strong, and her discontent with her marriage would be experienced with even greater intensity. She thus gave Larry mixed messages. She encouraged him to be more available to the kids but then, without being aware of it, undermined his tentative attempts to do so. Larry, in a similar fashion, gave Sandra the same "Please change!" and "Change back!" messages.

Toward the end of marital therapy, Sandra was able to do different steps in _this_ dance, too. As she became increasingly invested in fostering her own growth and development, she became less tightly enmeshed with her children and no longer looked to them to fill up the emptiness she had been experiencing. Sandra's earlier focus on her husband and children had protected her from confronting some difficult questions: "What are my priorities right now?" "Are there interests and skills that I would like to develop?" "What are my personal goals over the next several years?" As Sandra began to put her energy into struggling with these difficult issues, she was better able to allow Larry to relate to the children in his own way without correcting him or getting in the middle. As Sandra backed off, Larry moved in. The children, too, sensed that their mother was putting her energy into her own life and no longer needed them to be "loyal" to her as the "number-one" parent. Thus, they became freer to be close with their dad without anxiety and guilt. This was a difficult shift for Larry, because he was faced head on with his own worries about being a father and his concerns about his competence in this area.

TRYING TO CHANGE HIM

Sandra had spent many years trying to change Larry. "If only he would change!" "If only he would be different!" She truly believed that a change in Larry would secure her happiness. But the more Sandra put her energies into trying to change and control Larry, the more things stayed the same. For trying to change or control another person is a solution that never, never works. And while Sandra poured all that effort into trying to change someone she could not change, she failed to exercise the power that *was* hers—*the power to change her own self.*

Sandra's realization that she could not change Larry did not mean that she silently swallowed her anger and dissatisfaction. If anything, she learned to articulate her reactions to Larry with clarity and assurance. She was aware, however, that in response to these statements of her own wishes and preferences, Larry would change or not change. And if he did *not* change, it was Sandra's job to decide what *she* would or would not do from there. This is something more difficult than participating in further fighting that only maintains the status quo.

For example, Larry's pattern of leaving household jobs half finished was a real irritant to Sandra. The typical old pattern was that Sandra would push Larry to finish a task, in response to which he would procrastinate further, which provoked Sandra into pushing harder. The circular dance was procrastinate-push-procrastinate-push . . . Sandra would continue to try to *make* Larry finish the job despite the likelihood that it would not get done.

As is often the case, Sandra's pushing actually helped Larry to be more comfortable with his irresponsible behavior. He would become angry and defensive in the face of her criticisms, which protected him from feeling guilty and concerned about his difficulty completing tasks. Sandra's attempts to change Larry only made it easier for him to avoid confronting his own problem.

Now, Sandra is clear in telling Larry that she becomes upset when the bathroom ceiling remains half painted and buckets of paint are lying around the house. If Larry shows no positive response to her complaint, Sandra then puts her energy into determining what she will do or will not do in order to take care of her own needs. She is able to do this when she *begins* to feel resentful, so that her anger does not build up. Thus, she can talk to Larry without hostility and let him know that she is needing to do something *for* herself and not *to* him.

After considering the options open to her, she may choose to say any number of things to Larry. It may be: "Okay, I don't like it, but I can live with it." Or: "Larry, I would rather you finish what you began, but if you are unable to do so this week, it is bothersome enough to me that I will do it myself. I can paint it without becoming angry, so that's okay with me." Or: "I can only tolerate looking at this unfinished job for one week, and I can't complete it myself without becoming angry about it. So, what might we do that you don't feel pushed and I don't become furious? One idea I have is to call the painter if it's not done by Saturday." Obviously, there is *something* Sandra can do about the ceiling, for if Larry were to disappear from the earth, it is highly unlikely that she would live out the rest of her life with a half-painted ceiling. In the old pattern, however, Sandra put so much effort into trying to change Larry that she obscured from herself her own power to act and make choices. And this, in the end, is the only real power we have.

4

ANGER AT OUR IMPOSSIBLE MOTHERS
The Story of Maggie

Turning theory and good intentions into practice is especially challenging with members of our first family. Our relationships with our parents and siblings are the most influential in our lives and they are never simple. Families tend to establish rigid rules and roles that govern how each member is to think, feel, and behave, and these are not easily challenged or changed. When one individual in a family begins to behave in a new way that does not conform to the old family scripts, anxiety skyrockets and before long everyone is trying to reinstate the old familiar patterns.

Rather than face the strong feelings of anxiety and discomfort that are inevitably evoked when we clarify a new position in an old relationship, we may instead do the very two things with our anger that only serve to block the possibility that change will occur.

First, we may "confront" members of our family by telling them what's wrong with them and how they should think, feel, or behave differently. That is, we try to change the *other* person. This other person typically (and understandably) becomes upset and defensive. We then become frustrated or guilty and allow things to return to the usual pattern. "My mother (father, sister, brother) can't change!" is our subsequent conclusion.

Second, we may cut ourselves off from our parents or siblings emotionally and/or geographically. Surely, the fastest cure for chronic anger or frustration is simply to leave home, to move across the country (better yet, to a different country), or to find a sympathetic therapist who will "re-parent" us. We can keep family visits few and far between or we can keep them polite and superficial. True enough, such distancing does bring short-term relief by lowering the anxiety and emotional intensity in these relationships and freeing us of the uncomfortable feelings that may be evoked upon closer emotional contact. The problem is that there is a long-term cost. All the unresolved emotional intensity is likely to get played out in another important relationship, such as that with a spouse, a lover, or, if we ourselves are parents, a child. No less important is the fact that emotional distancing from our first family prevents us from proceeding calmly and clearly in new relationships. When we learn to move differently in our family and get "unstuck" in these important relationships, we will function with greater satisfaction in every relationship we are in. And, as Maggie's story illustrates, we *can* go home again. We can learn to do something different with our anger.

THE WAY IT WAS

Maggie, a twenty-eight-year-old graduate student at a local university, came to see me because of her recurrent migraine headaches and her lack of sexual interest in her husband, Bob. Beginning with our first therapy session, however, she maintained an almost single-minded focus on her mother. Although Maggie lived in Kansas and her mother in California, time and space had healed no wounds.

Maggie had no problem getting in touch with her anger at her mother, and if left to herself, she spoke of little else. From Maggie's description, she and her mother had never gotten along well, nor had their relationship improved when Maggie left home and started a family of her own. Maggie's mother and father were divorced five years prior to her starting therapy, shortly after she married Bob and moved away from the west coast. Since that time, Maggie and her father had become increasingly distant, while her relationship with her mother had become more intense, even though they were physically apart.

Maggie dutifully invited her mother for annual visits, but by the third day Maggie would feel frustration and rage. During her therapy sessions, she would describe the horrors of the particular visit to which she was being subjected. With despair and anger in her voice, she would recite her mother's crime sheet, which was endless. In vivid detail, she would document her mother's unrelenting negativism and intrusiveness. During one visit, for example, Maggie reported the following events: Maggie and Bob had redecorated their living room; mother hadn't noticed. Bob had just learned of his forthcoming promotion; mother didn't comment. Maggie and Bob effortfully prepared fancy dinners; mother complained that the food was too rich. To top it all off, mother lectured Maggie about her messy kitchen and criticized her management of money. And when Maggie announced that she was three months pregnant, mother replied, "How will you deal with a child when you can hardly make time to clean your house?"

About all this, Maggie had said nothing, except for a few sarcastic comments and one enormous blowup to mark the day of her mother's departure. Maggie was furious and she saw therapy as a place where she could safely vent her anger. But that's about all she did. She did not, for example, say to her mother, "Mom, this pregnancy means a great deal to Bob and me. We're excited about it, and although I worry sometimes, I'm confident that we'll do just fine." Nor did she say, "Mother, I know that I manage money in a way that's very different from your way. But what I do is working okay for me, just as your way works for you." Instead, Maggie tended to keep quiet when she felt unappreciated or put down. She alternated between seething silently, emotionally distancing herself, and finally blowing up. None of these reactions was helpful to her.

Obviously, it is not necessary, or even desirable, to personally address every injustice and irritation that comes our way. It can be an act of maturity to let something go. But for Maggie, not speaking up—and then blowing up—had become the painful rule in her relationship with mother. Maggie was de-selfing herself by failing to address issues that mattered to her, and as a result, she felt angry, frustrated, victimized, and depressed.

When I asked Maggie about her silences, she provided countless justifications for her failure to speak up. Among them were: "I could never say that!" "My mother can't hear." "It would only make things worse." "I've tried it a hundred times and it doesn't work." "The situation is hopeless." "It would kill my mother if I said that." "It's just not important enough to me anymore." "You just don't know my mother!"

Sound familiar? When emotional intensity is high in a family, most of us put the entire responsibility for poor communication on the other person. It is one's mother/father/sister/brother who is deaf, defensive, crazy, hopeless, helpless, fragile, or set in their ways. Always, we perceive that it is the *other* who prevents us from speaking and keeps the relationship from changing. We disown our own part in the interactions we complain of and, with it, our power to bring about a change.

Maggie acted as if her only options were either to keep quiet or to argue and fight, although she knew from experience that neither worked. Indeed, when she did vent her anger, the result left her feeling so frustrated that she would begin yet another cycle of silence and emotional withdrawal.

ONE YEAR LATER: GOING TO BATTLE

Amy—Maggie and Bob's new baby—was two months old when Maggie's mother made her next visit. Tensions between the two women were already sky high by the time mother's suitcase was unpacked, and only seemed to escalate as the visit progressed. Having a new baby brought out the fighter in Maggie, and she and her mother were constantly locking horns, especially on the subject of Amy's care.

When Maggie decided to let Amy cry herself to sleep, her mother suggested that she be picked up, insisting that such neglect might have potentially damaging effects. When Maggie nursed her baby on demand, her mother advised her to nurse on a fixed schedule and warned that Maggie was spoiling Amy by overly long feedings. And so it went.

On this particular visit, Maggie did not sit still through her mother's lectures and criticisms. Armed with supporting evidence from physicians, psychologists, and child-care experts, Maggie set out to prove her wrong on every count. She debated her mother constantly. The more thoroughly Maggie martialed her evidence, the more tenaciously her mother clung to her own opinions. When finally this sequence reached an intolerable point, Maggie would angrily accuse her mother of being rigid, controlling, and unable to listen. Her mother would then become sullen and withdrawn, in response to which Maggie retreated into silence. Things would settle down for a while and then the fighting would begin again.

Four days into the visit, Maggie reported that her nerves were on edge and she was at the tail end of a migraine headache. She once again diagnosed her mother as "a hopeless case" and stated bitterly that she had no option but to retreat to her earlier style of silent suffering and to see her mother as little as possible in the future.

What Went Wrong?

One problem with Maggie's style of fighting with her mother may already be obvious: Maggie was trying to change her mother rather than clearly state her own beliefs and convictions and stand behind them. To attempt to change another person, particularly a parent, is a self-defeating move. Predictably, Maggie's mother would only cling with greater determination to her own beliefs in the face of her daughter's pressuring her to admit error. Maggie had yet to learn that she cannot control or change another person's thoughts and feelings. Her attempts to do so in fact provoked the very rigidity in her mother that she found so disturbing.

Perhaps the reader can identify a second problematic aspect of Maggie's fights with her mother. Maggie had not yet identified the true source of her anger. As is often the case, mother and daughter were fighting about a pseudo issue. Arguing about such child-rearing practices as feeding Amy on schedule or demand, or rocking her to sleep rather than letting her cry it out, only masks the *real* issue here: Maggie's independence from her mother.

Maggie's intense reactivity to her mother also prevented her from being able to think about her situation in a clear, focused way. Until she can calm down enough to become more reflective, she is unlikely to identify her main problem and decide how she wants to deal with it. Simply giving vent to stored-up anger has no particular therapeutic value. Such catharsis may indeed offer feelings of relief—especially for the person doing the venting—and the accused party usually survives the verbal onslaught. But this solution can only be temporary.

Taking Stock of the Situation

During one particular psychotherapy hour when Maggie was describing yet another frustrating battle with mother on some question of Amy's care, I decided to interrupt her:

"You know, I'm struck by your protectiveness of your mother," I remarked.

"Protectiveness?" exclaimed Maggie, looking at me as if I had surely gone mad. "She's driving me crazy. I'm not protecting her! I'm fighting with her constantly."

"And what's the outcome of these fights?" It was a rhetorical question.

"Nothing! Nothing ever changes!" Maggie declared.

"Exactly," I said. "And that is how you protect her. By

participating in fights that lead nowhere and never speaking directly to the real issue. You fight with your mother rather than let her know where you stand."

"Where I stand on what?" asked Maggie.

"Where you stand on the question of who is in charge of your baby and who has the authority to make decisions about her care."

Maggie was silent for a long moment. The anger on her face changed slowly to a look of mild depression and concern. "Maybe I'm not sure where I stand."

"Perhaps, then," I responded, "we had better take a look at that issue first."

After this exchange, Maggie began to move in a new direction. She began to *think* carefully about her situation, as opposed to expressing feelings about it, and to clarify where *she* stood, rather than continuing to criticize her mother. In this process, Maggie gained a new perspective on her pattern of relating to her mother. To her surprise, she discovered that she felt guilty about excluding her mother from her new family; part of her wanted to "share" her children so that her mother would not feel left out or depressed. Maggie thought about her parents' divorce, which followed on the heels of her own marriage to Bob, and she wondered out loud whether her leaving home and getting married were somehow linked to the ending of her parents' marriage. She then revealed a critical piece of information that she had failed to mention in all of our time working together: her mother had received electroshock therapy for a post-partum depression following Maggie's birth. Although Maggie was not at first aware of it, she was worried that following the event of Amy's birth, her mother would again become depressed.

In the months that followed, Maggie explored many facets of the deep bond between herself and her mother. She began to feel less angry and more empathic toward her mother as she understood better how every member of the family, including herself, had unconsciously tried to protect her mother from loneliness and depression whether, in reality, she wanted this protection or not. More important, Maggie was able to recognize her own wish to maintain the status quo—to hold on to her mother and be close in the old ways. And as long as Maggie chose to fight, or to remain silent on issues that mattered to her, she would never really leave home. Even if she moved to the moon, she would still be her mother's little girl.

As Maggie became less scared and guilty about showing her mother her own strong and separate self, she became more ready to make a change in this relationship. She was no longer going to participate in the same old fights. Nor would she sit silently seething when she felt that her authority as both a mother and an adult woman was being questioned. Maggie was going to demonstrate her independence.

BREAKING A PATTERN—MOTHER'S NEXT VISIT

Amy was almost a year and half now. It was a hot Sunday afternoon, the second day of Maggie's mother's visit, and Bob was out playing tennis with his friends. Maggie had just put Amy down for a nap and she was crying in her crib. Only five minutes had passed when her mother suddenly jumped up from her chair, scooped Amy out of the crib, and said to Maggie, "I just can't stand to hear her cry! I'm going to rock her to sleep!"

Anger welled up inside Maggie and for a moment she

felt like yelling at her mother. But she was now aware that fighting was a way of protecting both her mother and herself. And silence was the same. For both fighting and silence would insure that Maggie would never declare her independence from her mother. Suddenly, she simmered down.

With as much poise as Maggie could muster, she stood up, lifted Amy from her mother's arms, and placed her gently back in the crib. Then she turned to her mother and said, without anger or criticism in her voice, "Mom, let's go out on the porch. I really want to talk with you about something important to me."

Maggie's heart was beating so fast, it occurred to her that she might faint. She realized in a split second that it would be easier to fight than to do what she needed to do. She was about to show her mother her separateness and independence. And she was going to proceed to do so in a mature and responsible fashion. Her mother was clearly nervous, too; it was unlike her daughter to speak to her in a calm but firm manner.

The two women were seated on the porch swing. Maggie's mother spoke first, with anger that barely masked the anxiety in her voice: "Margaret" (it was the name her mother had always used when she was upset with Maggie), "I cannot stand to hear that child cry. When a child needs to be picked up, I just can't sit there pretending I don't hear her screaming."

Maggie's voice was level and sure. She looked at her mother directly and spoke without anger. "Mom," she said, "I appreciate how concerned you are about Amy. I know it's important to you that your grandchildren are well-cared-for. But there's something I feel I must tell you. . . ."

Maggie paused for a moment. She felt an icy fear in her

chest without knowing why. She guessed that her mother felt it, too. But she kept her composure.

"You see, Mom, Amy is *my* child. And I'm struggling hard to learn to be a good mother and to establish a good relationship with her. It's very important to me that with *my* child, I do what *I* think is right. I know that sometimes I'll make mistakes, sometimes I'll do the wrong thing. But right now I need to take care of Amy in a way that *I* see fit. I need to do that for her and I need to do that for me. And I very much want to have your support in that." Maggie heard the strength and maturity in her own voice and it surprised her. She continued with a warmth that was beginning to feel genuine: "Mom, when you tell me what to do with Amy, or correct me, or take things into your own hands, it's not helpful to me. It would mean a whole lot to me if you would not do that anymore."

There was a moment of dead silence. Maggie felt as if she had stabbed her mother with a knife. Then her mother's voice came back, familiar and angry. It was as if she had not heard:

"Maggie, I cannot stand to see that child suffer. A child of Amy's age must not be left to sob uncontrollably in her crib." Mother continued to speak at length about the adverse psychological effects of Maggie's practice.

Maggie was tempted to bolster her own position, but she refrained from doing so. Arguing, she realized, deflected attention from the issue Maggie was at last beginning to speak to—that of her being a separate and different person from her mother, with her own unique way of being in the world.

Maggie listened patiently and respectfully until her mother was through. She did not contradict her, nor did she fight back. Maggie was doing something very different, and both she and her mother knew it.

"Mom," Maggie said softly, "I don't think you're hearing me. Perhaps I'm wrong about the question of Amy's crying in her crib, or perhaps I'm right. I can't know for sure. But what's most important to me right now is that, as Amy's mother, I do what *I* feel is best. I'm not saying that I'll never make mistakes or that I have the final word on things. What I am saying is that I'm working hard to be independent and to gain confidence in myself as Amy's mother. It's very important to me that with *my* child, I do what *I* think is right."

Her mother became more anxious and upped the ante: "I've raised four children. Are you telling me that you don't want any advice at all? That I have nothing worthwhile to say? Are you saying that I should have stayed home? I can leave, you know, if I'm just in the way. It sounds like I've been making things worse rather than better!"

Maggie felt a new wave of anger rising up, but this time it disappeared quickly. Maggie had her feet on the ground. She knew she was not going to accept the invitation to fight, and thus reinstate old patterns. Instead, she said, "Mother, I very much appreciate your being here. I'm aware how much you know about raising children. And maybe at some point when I am more secure in my own independence and my own mothering skills, I'll be asking you for some advice."

"But you don't want my advice now?" It was more an accusation than a question.

"That's right, Mother," Maggie answered. "Unless I specifically ask for advice, I don't want it."

"I can't stand by and watch you ruin that child." Maggie's mother was becoming more irrational and provocative, unconsciously trying to draw Maggie back into fighting in order to reinstate their earlier, predictable relationship.

"You know, Mother," Maggie said, "Bob and I have our struggles as parents. But I think that we're pretty good at it and that we'll get better. I'm confident that we won't ruin Amy."

"And you're just criticizing me!" Mother continued, as if Maggie had not just spoken. "I've been trying to help you and you just throw it back in my face!"

"Mom"—Maggie's voice was still calm—"I'm not criticizing you. I'm not saying that you're doing the wrong thing. I'm sharing *my* reaction. When you do something like pick up Amy when I put her down, I get upset because I'm trying to develop my confidence as a mother on my own. I'm not criticizing you. I am sharing with you how I feel and what I want."

Maggie's mother rose abruptly and went back into the house, slamming the screen door behind her. Maggie had the terrifying fantasy that her mother was going to kill herself and that she would never see her again. Suddenly, Maggie noticed that her own knees were shaking and she felt dizzy. Both Maggie and her mother were experiencing "separation anxiety." Maggie was beginning to leave home.

UNDERSTANDING MOTHER'S REACTION

When Maggie stepped out of her characteristic position in her relationship with her mother, she experienced a panicky feeling about herself and her mother's well-being. Her mother responded to Maggie's changed style of communication by intensifying her own position, almost to absurd proportions, in a powerful effort to protect both herself and her daughter from the strong anxiety that standing on one's own can evoke in parties who are close to each other.

What might at first glance appear to be an obnoxious, unfeeling response on her mother's part reflects her deep wish to stay close to her daughter and to spare them both the painful solitude of greater separateness and independence. Indeed, if her mother had been able to respond calmly and rationally, Maggie herself would have been left to experience even more of the separation anxiety that welled up in her from time to time during their talk. Adding to each woman's deep-seated fear of losing the other was the fact that their old pattern of interaction was so long standing, neither Maggie nor her mother knew a different way of relating. Precisely what kind of relationship could replace this one was a scary unknown to both of them. Thus, when Maggie broke the old repetitive pattern of communicating, her mother, unconsciously sensing a threat to their relationship, rallied to keep it intact.

Although Maggie was intellectually prepared for the sequence of events that occurred, she still found herself feeling shaken and depressed. "Have I made a mistake?" she asked herself. "Is my mother acting crazy?" "Will I lose my mother forever just because I finally had the courage to state my own point of view?"

The answer is no. Countermoves are par for the course when we begin to define a stronger self in a family relationship. Maggie's mother's "Change back!" reaction was her way of communicating that Maggie's act of independence—her statement of self—was a cruel rejection of her. The threats—some overt, some disguised—were that her mother would become depressed, that she would withdraw, that she would fall apart, and that the relationship between her and Maggie would be severed. As we have seen, this powerful emotional counterforce ("You're wrong"; "Change back!"; "Or else . . .") is predictable, understandable, and, to some extent, universal. What happens next is up to Maggie.

A New Dance—One Step at a Time

Maggie's work had just begun. As her mother angrily retreated to her room, Maggie felt scared and guilty. More than anything, she wanted to get away from her mother—to "leave the field." She had said what she needed to say and now her only wish was that she or her mother would disappear.

It doesn't work. "Hit-and-run" confrontation in an important relationship does not lead to lasting change. If Maggie is really serious about change, she still has a challenging road to walk.

First, Maggie needs to show (for her own sake as well as her mother's) that at last she is declaring her separateness and independence from mother, but that she is *not* declaring a lack of caring or closeness. *Independence means that we clearly define our own selves on emotionally important issues, but it does not mean emotional distance.* Thus, Maggie needs to show, through her behavior, that although she will stand behind her own wants and convictions, she is still her mother's daughter and loves her mother very much.

The work of negotiating greater independence—especially between a mother and a daughter—may be so fraught with mutual anxieties about rejection and loss that the person making the move (in this case, Maggie) must be responsible for maintaining emotional contact with the other (her mother). If Maggie fails in this regard, her mother will feel rejected and upset; Maggie will feel anxious and guilty; and both mother and daughter will unconsciously agree to return their relationship to the old predictable pattern.

How can Maggie best maintain emotional closeness with her mother at this time? She might ask her mother questions about her interests and activities. She can express interest in learning more about her mother's own past and personal history. This is one of the best ways to stay emotionally connected to members of our family and, at the same time, learn more about our selves (see Chapter 6). When things cool off a bit and the relationship is calm, Maggie might initiate a dialogue with her mother on the subject of raising children—an area in which mother has valuable expertise. For example, Maggie might say, "You know, Mother, sometimes I try to comfort Amy and she keeps crying and crying. Did you go through that when we were little? How did you handle it?" Or, "What was it like for you to raise four children, especially when two of us were only a year apart?" If her mother were to reply in a huff, "Well, I thought *you* had enough of *my* advice!" Maggie might respond, "Actually, I don't find advice helpful—even good advice—because I need to struggle with the problem myself and find my own solution. But I do find it very useful to learn more about your own experience and how you handled things." Blocking advice-giving—if that is one of the problems—is not the same as cutting off the lines of communication. As we become more independent we learn *more* about our family members, not less, and we are able to share more about our selves.

In addition to the task of being the caretaker in maintaining emotional contact, Maggie will now face a series of "tests," for her mother will need to determine whether Maggie really "means it," or whether she is willing to return to the previous pattern of interaction. Again, this is not because Maggie's mother is a rigid, crazy woman, but because this is the predictable reaction in all family systems. It is as basic as a law of physics. Maggie must be prepared to have her mother attack, withdraw, threaten, and "do her old thing" with Maggie's baby, Amy. And she must be equally prepared to restate her convictions like a broken record if necessary, yet retain emotional contact with her mother as best she can. The point cannot be emphasized enough: No successful move toward greater independence occurs in one "hit-and-run" confrontation.

And so, Maggie's work was far from over at the point when her mother rose and retreated to her room. On this particular day, Maggie had only begun the process of attaining a higher level of separateness from her first family. If she can stay on course, over time she will achieve greater independence and clarity of self that will manifest itself in all her important relationships. Her mother, too, is likely to shift to a more separate mode of interacting and to proceed in her own life with greater emotional maturity.

Will Maggie be able to tolerate the anxiety and guilt associated with clarifying a more independent self, or will she become so emotionally caught up in her mother's reactions as to lapse back into the reassuringly familiar fights that kept her and her mother close in the old way? The ball is in Maggie's court. And the difficult choice is hers.

Together, Differently

As it happened, Maggie chose to work on changing the old pattern. She fell on her face many times and temporarily slipped back into fighting, instructing, criticizing her mother, or distancing herself from the relationship. But most important, she was able to pick herself up each time and get back on course. She continued to make her declaration of independence with increasingly less blaming and distancing as time progressed. In doing so, she established a new, more adult relationship with her mother and began to talk with her about topics that had previously been eclipsed by their endless years of fighting. Maggie began to ask her mother more about her past life, about her own mother and father and her childhood and memorable events. She even initiated discussions about subjects that had formerly been "taboo" ("Mom, how do you understand that you got so depressed after I was born?"). Maggie talked with her mother in a way that neither of them had previously done, since their interactions were so heavily based on silence, sarcasm, outright fighting, and emotional distancing. As they talked more and more often in this new way, Maggie was able to see her mother's old "obnoxious" behaviors in a different light. She came to appreciate that her mother's apparent intrusiveness and criticism were in fact expressions of her own wish to be helpful to her daughter, as well as her fear that were she not, she would lose Maggie. Besides advising and criticizing, her mother had been as bewildered as Maggie about how to be helpful and close. She, too, sensed Maggie's need not to let go—to hold on in the old ways. Maggie also learned that her mother had had much the same kind of relationship with *her* mother, maintaining closeness through constant squabbling.

And what about Maggie's father? Like many fathers, he was most conspicuous by his absence. Maggie's distant relationship with her father had become even more pronounced following her parents' divorce, in part because of an unspoken family rule that Maggie was to be her mother's "ally" as her parents negotiated the divorce. When Maggie herself no longer needed to maintain her special bond with mother in the old way, she began working on having an adult, one-to-one relationship with her father as well.

This was not an easy task, because both Maggie and her father had a good share of anxiety and discomfort about establishing an emotionally close relationship. When Maggie first began to write to her dad, he reacted by distancing himself further, which was one of a number of countermoves, in response to her initiating a change. Indeed, her father's "Change back!" reactions were as dramatic as her mother's, although they took a different form. Much to Maggie's credit, she was able to maintain a calm, nonreactive position and she persisted, in a low-keyed way, to write to him and share the important events and issues going on in her life. Although mother and father were still fighting it out, Maggie's new level of independence helped her to stay out of the conflicts between them—a feat that required considerable assertiveness on her part. Over time, her relationship with her father developed and deepened.

As a result of the changes that Maggie made with her mother and father, she became free of the symptoms that first brought her to see me. Her headaches did not return and she became more sexually responsive with her husband, Bob. She also felt clearer and more assertive in all of her other relationships.

The work that Maggie did will have reverberations in the next generation. When her children are older, she will be better able to allow them the appropriate degree of independence and separateness, for the degree of independence that we achieve from our own family of origin is always played out in the following generation. Had Maggie not done this work, she would in time have found herself overinvolved and intensely reactive to one or more of her children. Or, alternatively, she might have been overly distant and emotionally cut off when her children were grown, which is simply the other side of the same coin. Although Maggie is not yet aware of it, the work that she did is the best "parent-effectiveness training" that money can buy.

BECOMING OUR OWN PERSON

Autonomy, separateness, independence, selfhood—these are all concepts that psychotherapists embrace as primary values and goals. And so do the women who seek help: "I want to find myself." "I want to discover who I really am and what I want." "I don't want to be so concerned with other people's approval." "I want to have a close relationship and still be my own person."

The task of defining (and maintaining) a separate self within our closest relationships is one that begins in our first family but does not end there. Like Maggie, we can proceed to work on achieving greater independence (and with it, an increased capacity for intimacy and togetherness) at any stage of our lives. Renegotiating relationships with persons on our own family tree yields especially rich rewards, because the degree of self that we carve out in this arena will greatly influence the nature of our current relationships.

In this lifelong task of forging a clear self, our anger is a double-edged sword. On the one hand, it helps to preserve our integrity and self-regard. Maggie's anger at her mother was the signal that let her know she was not comfortable in the old pattern of relating to her mother and that she needed to make a change. However, as we have seen, venting anger does not solve the problem that anger signals. To the contrary, Maggie's success at becoming her own separate person rested on her ability to share something about herself with her mother and father in a straightforward, nonblaming way while maintaining emotional contact with them throughout the process. It required, also, that Maggie uphold her position with persistence and calm, without getting emotionally buffeted about by the inevitable countermoves and "Change back!" reactions we meet whenever we assume a more autonomous position in an important relationship. This is what achieving selfhood and independence is all about. And it requires, among other things, a particular way of talking and a degree of clarity that are especially difficult to achieve when we are angry.

5

USING ANGER AS A GUIDE
The Road to a Clearer Self

I was first introduced to the notion of turning anger into "I messages" some years back when I read Thomas Gordon's best-selling book, *Parent Effectiveness Training*. I still recall the first time I put his theory into practice. I was standing in the kitchen washing dishes when I noticed my son, Matthew, who was then three, sitting at the kitchen table about to cut an apple with a sharp knife. The conversation that followed went something like this:

ME: "Matthew, put that knife down. You're going to cut yourself."

MATTHEW: "No, I'm not."

ME (getting angry): "Yes, you are!"

MATTHEW (getting angrier): "No, I'm not!"

ME (even louder): "Yes, you are! Put it down!"

MATTHEW: "No!"

At this point in the escalating power struggle, I remembered what I had read about "I" messages. Every "you" message (for example, "You're going to cut yourself") could

88

be turned into an "I" message—that is, a nonblaming statement about one's own self. So, in a split second's time, I made the conversion:

"Matthew," I said again (this time without anger), "when I see you with that sharp knife, I feel scared. I am worried that you will cut yourself." At this point Matthew paused, looked me straight in the eye, and said calmly, "That's _your_ problem." To which I replied, "You're absolutely right. It _is_ my problem that I'm scared and I'm going to take care of my problem right now by taking that knife away from you." And so I did.

What was interesting to me was that Matthew relinquished the knife easily, without the usual anger and struggle and with no loss of pride. I was taking the knife away from him because I was worried, and exercised my parental authority in that light. I owned the problem ("I feel scared") and I took responsibility for my feelings. Later, I was to learn that Matthew had been cutting apples with a sharp knife for over a month in his Montessori preschool, but that is beside the point. What is important is that I was able to shift from "You're going to cut yourself" (did I have a crystal ball?) to "It _is_ my problem. . . ."

Of course, no one talks in calm "I messages" all the time. When my husband broke my favorite ceramic mug that had been with me since college, I did not turn to him with perfect serenity and say, "You know, dear, when you knock my cup off the table, my reaction is to feel angry and upset. It would mean a great deal to me if you would be more careful next time." Instead, I cursed him and created a small scene. He apologized, and a few minutes later we were the best of friends again.

There is nothing inherently virtuous in using "I messages" in all circumstances. If our goal is simply to let someone know we're angry, we can do it in our own personal style, and our style may do the job, or at least makes us feel better.

If, however, our goal is to break a pattern in an important relationship and/or to develop a stronger sense of self that we can bring to all our relationships, it is essential that we learn to translate our anger into clear, nonblaming statements about our own self.

There are any number of self-help books and assertiveness-training courses that teach men and women how to change "You are ..." communications into "I feel ..." communications. Certainly we maximize the opportunity for constructive dialogue if we say "I feel like I'm not being heard" rather than "You don't know how to listen." The story of how Maggie changed her relationship with her mother is a vivid illustration of this point. Shaping up our communication, however, is only a small part of the picture.

The more significant issue for women is that we may not have a clear "I" to communicate about, and we are not prepared to handle the intense negative reactions that come our way when we do begin to define and assert the self.

As we have seen, women often fear that having a clear "I" means *threatening* a relationship or *losing* an important person. Thus, rather than using our anger as a challenge to think more clearly about the "I" in our relationships, we may, when angry, actually blur what personal clarity we *do* have. And we may do this not only under our own roof with intimate others but on the job as well with office mates. Karen's difficulty maintaining a clear "I" will ring a bell for those of us who have occasion to fall into the "nice lady" category at work.

FROM ANGER TO TEARS

Karen was one of two young women who sold life insurance in an otherwise all-male firm. After her first year on the job, she received a written evaluation from her boss that placed her in the "Very Satisfactory" performance range. From Karen's perspective, her work was in the "Superior" range. By objective criteria, her sales record was right at the top.

This evaluation meant much to Karen, since only employees rated "Superior" received a special salary bonus along with the opportunity to attend out-of-state seminars. Karen was raising two children with little financial support from her ex-husband. She needed the money and wanted the educational opportunities that would allow her to advance.

When Karen brought her story to group psychotherapy, she had tears in her eyes. "I'm hurt," said Karen. "It's just not fair!" When asked what she planned to do, Karen said flatly, "Nothing." As she put it, "It's just not worth the hassle."

"Aren't you angry?" a group member inquired. "Why should I be angry?" responded Karen. "Where will it get me? It only makes things worse." These were the things that Karen would predictably say to avoid taking her anger seriously.

With help from the other group members, Karen was finally able to acknowledge her anger and mobilize the courage to meet with her boss to discuss the evaluation. She got off to a good start with him by lucidly stating why she believed she deserved the higher rating. At first, her boss seemed to listen attentively, but it soon became evident that he was feeling defensive and wasn't really considering her view of the matter. When she finished talking, he brushed aside the valid points that she had made and began instead to focus on certain problems that he had noticed in *her* work. These problems, although real, were trivial and unrelated to the question of whether or not Karen deserved a "Superior" rating. Then he added that "other people" in the office thought she was "a little rough around the edges."

"What do you mean?" asked Karen.

"Perhaps it's a personality issue," he continued, "but you give the impression to some people that you are less committed to your work than you might be."

At this point, Karen's eyes filled with tears and she felt totally inarticulate. "I don't understand that," she said softly, doing her best not to burst out crying. She then proceeded to tell her boss how unappreciated she felt because she was struggling so hard to raise two children and to succeed in a full-time job as well. Now that tears and "hurt" had replaced Karen's calm assertiveness, her boss shifted from defensiveness to paternalistic concern. He reassured Karen that she showed a great deal of potential in her work, and he empathized with the difficult task of being a single parent. The meeting ended with Karen's sharing some of the emotional struggles she was having since her divorce, while her boss lent a sympathetic ear. She did not mention anything further about the evaluation, nor did he. Karen left the office feeling relieved that she had not alienated her boss and that their meeting had ended on a warm note.

When Karen told us her story at the next group-therapy session, she concluded with the following words: "You see— it doesn't do any good to confront him. He doesn't listen. Anyway, the evaluation is really no big deal. To tell the truth, it really doesn't matter that much to me."

But the other group members did not drop the subject

so easily. They had a number of questions for Karen that forced her to confront her own uncertainty.

Who were these "other people" in the office who questioned Karen's commitment and who told the boss that she was "a little rough around the edges?"

Karen had no idea who her critics were.

What did "a little rough around the edges" mean?

Karen wasn't sure: "Something to do with my personality or character . . ."

What, specifically, would she have to do differently to get a "Superior" rating?

Karen didn't know.

It was not only that Karen failed to restate her position following her boss's initial defensiveness; she did not even allow herself to clarify the issues with him. She did not ask, "Who in the office is criticizing me?" Or, "Could you be more specific about my personality problems?" Or, "What, specifically, must I change in order to get a 'Superior' rating?" Karen's emotional reaction to her boss's criticism obscured her thinking about what she wanted to ask and what she wanted to say.

Feeling fuzzy-headed, inarticulate, and not so smart are common reactions experienced by women as we struggle to take a stand on our own behalf. *It is not just anger and fighting that we learn to fear; we avoid asking precise questions and making clear statements when we unconsciously suspect that doing so would expose our differences, make the other person fee: uncomfortable, and leave us standing alone.*

"But my boss *intimidates* me!" said Karen.

That's a cover story. Karen was really afraid of rocking the boat in an important relationship by persisting in her efforts to take up her own cause in a mature and articulate manner. Her tears and her willingness to let her boss play the role of advisor and confidant were, in part, her unconscious way of reinstating the status quo and apologizing for the "separateness" inherent in her initial position of disagreement. Karen's tears may also have been an unconscious attempt to make her boss feel guilty ("See how you've hurt me?")—a frequent practice for women who are blocked from making a direct statement of where we stand.

"But I'm not angry about it anymore," protested Karen. "It just doesn't matter."

Of *course* Karen is still angry. She just doesn't recognize it. Anger is inevitable when we submit to unfair circumstances and when we protect another person at our own expense.

Karen's denial of her anger and her failure to stand behind her position had inevitable costs. She felt tired and less enthusiastic at work. Two weeks after her evaluation, Karen misplaced a folder of important forms and she was seriously reprimanded. This self-sabotaging act was perhaps an unconscious attempt to put herself in the role of the "bad guy" who did not really deserve the "Superior" evaluation, rather than stand firm in her opinion that her boss had failed to give her the evaluation that she believed she deserved.

DENYING ANGER: THE UNCONSCIOUS IN ACTION

Have you ever initiated a confrontation at work, only to transform your anger into tears, apologies, guilt, confusion, or self-criticism? Karen's behavior may well strike a familiar, if not universal, chord among women. How can we better understand some of the deeper, unconscious reasons why any of us would attempt to deny our anger and sacrifice one of our most precious possessions—our personal clarity?

The Fear of Destructiveness

Karen's failure to defend her position in an articulate and persistent fashion with her boss was a pattern in her personal relationships as well. The explanations that she gave herself were just the tip of the iceberg: "I get intimidated." "I just can't think straight when I'm dealing with an authority figure." "I guess I don't have faith in my own convictions." Karen *did* lose her confidence when her ideas were not given the stamp of other people's approval, but this lack of confidence masked a more serious problem: Karen was *afraid* to be clear about the correctness of her position, because she would then experience pressure to *continue* to take up her own cause. And to do this might make her the *target* of her boss's anger and disapproval. As Karen put it, a "real fight" might ensue.

This idea frightened Karen, partly for realistic reasons, such as the possibility that her work situation would become difficult and uncomfortable or that she might even be fired. Surely, fighting would escalate the tensions between Karen and her boss, making it even less likely that she would be heard. Reality aside, however, Karen had a deep unconscious fear that fighting might unleash her fantasied destructive potential, although it had never seen the light of day. If she lost control of her anger, would she destroy everything? It was as if Karen feared that the full venting of her outrage might cause the entire office building to go up in flames. Also, like most women, Karen had little practice expressing her anger in a controlled, direct, and effective fashion.

It is not surprising that Karen had deep-seated fears of her own omnipotent destructiveness and the vulnerability of men. Our very definitions of "masculinity" and "femininity" are based on the notion that women must function as nonthreatening helpmates and ego builders to men lest men feel castrated and weakened. The problem for Karen was that this irrational fear had a high cost. Not only did she avoid fighting; she also avoided asserting her viewpoint, requesting explanations from others, and stating her wants. All of the above fell into the category of potentially destructive acts that might hurt or diminish others.

The Fear of Separateness

As much as Karen feared a volcanic eruption, she had an even greater fear, also safely tucked away in her subconscious. Karen was afraid of transforming her anger into concise statements of her thoughts and feelings lest she evoke that disturbing sense of separateness and aloneness that we experience when we make our differences known and encourage others to do the same. Maggie, for example, felt this "separation anxiety" when she talked with her mother about her baby in a new, more adult way. Sandra felt it when she apologized to Larry for being so critical and assumed more responsibility to provide for her own happiness. Barbara *would* have felt it had she stopped fighting and calmly told her husband that she planned to go to the "anger" workshop.

Separation anxiety may creep up on us whenever we shift to a more autonomous, nonblaming position in a relationship, or even when we simply consider the possibility. Sometimes such anxiety is based on a realistic fear that if we assume a bottom-line stance ("I am sorry, but I will not do what you are asking of me"), we risk losing a relationship or a job. More often, and more crucially, separation anxiety is based on an underlying discomfort with separateness and individuality that has its roots in our early family experience, where the unspoken expectation may have been that we keep a lid on our expressions of self. Daughters are especially sensitive to such demands and may become far more skilled at protecting the relational "we" than asserting the autonomous "I."

Karen was not aware of her separation anxiety, but it led her to transform her initially clear and strong position into tears and hurt. Expressing hurt allowed her boss to be helpful and restored her sense of connectedness to him—which made her feel safe despite the self-betrayal involved in this transformation. Karen had a long-standing pattern of attempting to restore the togetherness of her relationships by crying, criticizing herself, becoming confused, or prematurely making peace. At the heart of the problem was the fact that Karen (like Maggie, in Chapter 4) needed to work harder at the task of clarifying her separateness and independence within her first family. If Karen can stay in contact with family members and make progress in this arena, she will find that she will proceed more effectively when she is angry at work and with less fear of standing separate and alone, on her own two feet.

Moving Differently

If Karen were to do it all over again, how might she transform her anger into productive action? First, she can better prepare herself to deal with her boss's countermoves, which in this case consisted of his indirectly criticizing her work and deflecting her from the issue. Karen shouldn't try to change or control his reactions (which is not possible, anyway). Nor should she allow herself to be controlled by them. She can simply stay on course by listening to what he has to say and then restating her initial position. There is nothing wrong with sounding like a broken record now and then.

What if Karen starts to feel tearful or emotionally intense during the interaction? If this happens, she can take time out to regain her composure: She can say, "I need a little time to sort my thoughts out. Let's set up another time to talk more about it."

What if her supervisor refuses to consider changing the evaluation? Karen can then begin to give some thought to her next move. She may request a third party to review her evaluation. She may simply say to her boss, "I don't like it, but I can live with it." She may ask for specific instructions on how she might secure a "Superior" evaluation the next time around. No matter how skilled Karen becomes in handling her anger, she cannot *make* her boss change his mind or ensure that justice will prevail. She *can* state her position, recognize her choices, and make responsible decisions on her own behalf. The calmer and clearer that Karen can be with her boss, the clearer *he* will become about his own perspective on the evaluation and what *he* will and will not do. Could it be that Karen unconsciously preferred to avoid this kind of clarity so as to maintain the image of her boss as a "good guy?"

Karen's story illustrates how our unconscious fears of destructiveness and of separateness may block us from maintaining our clarity and using our anger as a challenge to take a new position or action on our own behalf. In some instances, however, our problem is not the *fear* of clarity but the *absence* of it. That we are angry is obvious. But we may have little perspective on the "I," as a result of focusing exclusively on what the *other* person is doing to us. Here is a personal example:

THE FRYING-PAN STORY

During a visit some years ago from my older sister, Susan, the two of us set off to Macy's, where I planned to buy a non-stick frying pan. Without much forethought, I picked up a pan that looked fine to me and began to head over to the cashier. Before I could take two steps, my sister informed me that I was buying the wrong pan. Not only did the tone of Susan's voice express supreme confidence in her own judgment, but her advice was accompanied by a rather detailed and technical account regarding the problems with the particular finish I had selected—a subject about which I knew nothing and cared even less. My initial reaction was to be once again impressed by my big sister's encyclopedic mind, but, as she continued on, I felt a growing anger. Who asked for her opinion? Why did she always think she was right? Why did she behave like the world's expert on all subjects? I briefly toyed with the idea of bopping her on the head with the pan I had in hand, but resisted the impulse. Instead, I marched over to the cashier like a sullen and rebellious little sister and paid for the pan I had chosen myself. It proved to be of poor quality and short-lived—just as Susan had predicted.

An old saying tells us: "We teach what we most need to learn." When I was recounting the incident to my friend Marianne Ault-Riché, who conducts anger workshops with me, I was as far from personal clarity as any person could be. Why was I angry? The answer was simple: because my sister was so difficult! She had caused my anger by her opinionated style and by her need to be an expert on all matters. Everything I said to Marianne about my anger was a statement about my sister—not one word about my own self.

Marianne listened and then responded lightly, "I'd love to take your sister shopping along with me! I would have been fascinated to learn about different types of non-stick cookware. Susan is so knowledgeable!"

Marianne was speaking honestly. If she had been in my shoes, her reaction to Susan's knowledge and personality would have been entirely positive. Indeed, the very qualities that I was criticizing were those that endeared Susan to certain others, my parents included. At that moment, I recognized what is so obvious to me in other people—that my blaming stance was preventing me from gaining an understanding of my heated reaction.

What was it about Susan's advice-giving and expertise that annoyed me? Why was it a problem for me? What was the pattern in our relationship, and what was my participation in it? Only after I was able to reflect on these questions was I able to tell Susan what was bothering me, without implying that her personality or way of being in the world was at fault.

First, I used my anger as an incentive to sort out what I wanted and then to set a limit with my sister. As Maggie did with her mother, I clarified with Susan that I wanted her advice only when I asked for it. It was understandably difficult for Susan to accept that I would choose to avoid helpful and sound advice, since she herself would welcome it, solicited or not. To help explain the problem that I had receiving her advice, I told her a bit about my experience of being a younger sister:

"You know, Susan, all my life I've seen you as a brilliant star. I've always looked up to you as the person who had all the answers. I felt you knew everything and could do anything. And I felt I was in a one-down position, like I didn't have much to teach or to offer you in return. In fact, when I feel intimidated by your brilliance, I react by becoming even less competent.

"Our relationship is very important to me and I'm trying to work on getting things more in balance for myself. What I think will help me is to steer clear of my big sister's help and advice for a while. I know that may sound silly and ungrateful, because you are so good at being helpful, but that's what would be most useful to me at this time."

I was, in fact, asking my sister to make a change in her behavior. However, I was asking her to make a change not because her advice-giving was bad or wrong or excessive but rather because that would be helpful to me, in light of my reactions to big-sisterly advice—reactions for which I took full responsibility.

Sharing my dilemma with Susan (including my envy about her being the brilliant star in the family) was an important step in breaking out of an old overfunctioning-underfunctioning pattern in which Susan was in the role of the competent helper and I in that of the less competent helpee. In the past, the more Susan expressed enough wisdom and competence for the two of us, the more I would react by de-selfing myself into a state of conspicuous fuzzy-headedness. As I verbalized my wish to be able to provide something for my sister (rather than always being on the receiving end of her big-sisterly wisdom), Susan responded by sharing some of *her* problems with me, and it became evident to me, for the first time, that she valued my perspective. Over time, our relationship became more balanced and

I no longer felt myself to be at the bottom of the seesaw. Today, I do value her advice—solicited or not—on any number of subjects, non-stick cookware included.

Using our anger as a starting point to become more knowledgeable about the self does not require that we analyze ourselves and provide lengthy psychological explanations of our reactions, as I did with Susan. If I had not identified some long-standing relationship issues, I might simply have told my sister that I didn't want advice and really wasn't clear about why. The essential ingredient of this story is that I used my anger to clarify a request based on my own personal wants, and not because I sought to become an uninvited authority on how Susan should best conduct herself.

Anger is a tool for change when it challenges us to become more of an expert on the self and less of an expert on others.

TAKING A FIRM STAND

Learning to use our anger effectively requires some letting go—letting go of blaming that other person whom we see as causing our problems and failing to provide for our happiness; letting go of the notion that it is our job to change other people or tell them how they should think, feel, behave. Yet, this does not mean that we passively accept or go along with any behavior. In fact, a "live-and-let-live" attitude can signal a de-selfed position, if we fail to clarify what is and is not acceptable or desirable to us in a relationship. The main issue is *how* we clarify our position.

Recently I worked with a woman named Ruth who was furious over her husband's neglect of his health. He had received poor medical treatment for a serious leg problem that was worsening, and he had no plans to seek further help. Ruth expressed her anger by lecturing him on what he should do for himself and interpreting his feelings and behavior. ("You're being self-destructive." "You're neglecting yourself the way your father did." "You're denying your own fears," etc.) Her husband, in response, adopted an increasingly bland attitude toward his problem (which was understandable, since his wife was voicing enough worry for both of them) and became more dogmatic in his refusal to consider further treatment. It was an escalating circular dance in which Ruth's "I-know-what's-best-for-you" attitude only intensified her husband's willful assertion of his independence on this issue, which led to longer and more frequent lectures on Ruth's part about what he should do and what he was *really* feeling. Like many women, Ruth was becoming the emotional reactor *for* her man, while he played out the role of the emotional dumbbell.

It was a big step for Ruth to recognize that it was up to her husband to determine his own feelings, to choose his own risks, and to assume the primary responsibility for his own health. This was his job, not hers. But it was equally important for Ruth to take her anger seriously—to use it to clarify, first to herself and then to her husband, that she was unable to live with the status quo and go about business as usual.

Ruth made an important change when she talked to her husband about her own feelings instead of criticizing and instructing him. Ruth's father had died from a degenerative illness when she was twelve and she now found herself scared of losing her husband as well. Instead of focusing on her husband's "self-destructiveness" or "neglect," Ruth was able to request that her husband seek medical help because of her own needs and feelings. She explained that her fears and anxieties were so great that she could not go about her day-to-day activities as if nothing was happening. She did not blame her husband for her reaction, nor did she say that she knew what was best for him. Rather, Ruth was now sharing *her* problem with the situation and asking her husband to respect the intensity of her discomfort. He did agree to go to the doctor, although he made it perfectly clear that he was going for *her* sake, not his own.

When we use our anger to make statements about the self, we assume a position of strength, because no one can argue with our own thoughts and feelings. They may try, but in response, we need not provide logical arguments in our defense. Instead, we can simply say, "Well, it may seem crazy or irrational to you, but this is the way I see it." Of course, there is never a guarantee that other people will alter their behavior in the way that we want them to. Joan's story is illustrative.

A Bottom-Line Position

Joan and Carl had been living together for a year and had maintained their separate friendships with both sexes. They were in agreement that they were committed to monogamy, but did not want to sacrifice the opportunity to have close friends. This informal contract proved to be workable, until Carl began spending time with his young research assistant who was in the process of going through a divorce. In response, Joan found herself feeling jealous, threatened, and angry.

For almost a year the relationship between Carl and his assistant remained the focus of nonproductive fighting. Joan would question whether Carl's feelings were truly platonic and Carl, in turn, would accuse her of being paranoid and possessive. They had countless intellectual debates regarding boundary issues: Was it appropriate for Carl's assistant to call him at home in the evening to talk about her divorce? Was it okay for Carl to have dinner with her or just lunch? Joan shifted back and forth between blaming Carl and blaming herself, while nothing was resolved. Her recurrent anger, however, was a strong signal that despite the passage of time, she was not at peace with this relationship.

The turning point came when Joan stopped complaining about Carl's behavior and stated openly that the situation was not acceptable to her. She did not criticize him for doing something bad or wrong, and she even acknowledged that another woman in her shoes might not complain or might even welcome the opportunity to do the same herself. Joan's point was simply that she was experiencing more jealousy and anger than she could live with.

When Carl interpreted her reaction as "pathological" and "middle-class," Joan did not fight or become defensive. Instead she said, "Well, my feelings are my feelings. And I am having such a painful reaction to your relationship with this woman that I want you to end it. It may be ninety-nine percent my problem, but I'm unable to live with it and still feel okay about us. I'm just finding it too difficult." Joan upheld this position with dignity and firmness.

Joan's clarity about her emotional anguish forced Carl to clarify his own priorities—and his first priority was not Joan. Carl refused to end his relationship with his research assistant. Joan, after considerable personal turmoil, finally took a bottom-line position and said, "I can't continue to live with you if you continue in this relationship." She said this not as a threat or as an attempt at emotional blackmail but rather to share what she was experiencing and declare what was possible for her. Carl didn't respond and continued on as usual, and Joan requested that he move out. Soon afterward, Carl left Joan entirely and moved in with his research assistant.

Joan suffered a great deal; however, she felt good about the position she had taken. She had lost Carl, but she had saved her dignity and self-respect. Did she do the right thing? Joan did the right thing for Joan, but some of us in her place might have chosen to do something different—or not have known what to do at all.

In using our anger as a guide to determining our innermost needs, values, and priorities, we should not be distressed if we discover just how unclear we are. If we feel chronically angry or bitter in an important relationship, this is a signal that too much of the self has been compromised and we are uncertain about what new position to take or what options we have available to us. To recognize our lack of clarity is not a weakness but an opportunity, a challenge, and a strength.

There is no reason why women *should* be clear about the "I." "Who am I?" "What do I want?" "What do I deserve?" These are questions that we all struggle with—and for good reason. For too long, we have been encouraged *not* to question but to accept other-defined notions of our "true nature," our "appropriate place," our "maternal responsibilities," our "feminine role," and so forth. Or we have been taught to substitute other questions: "How can I please others?" "How can I win love and approval?" "How can I keep the peace?" We suffer most when we fail to grapple

with the "Who am I?" questions and when we deny feeling
the anger that signals that such questions are there for us to
consider.

It is an act of courage to acknowledge our own uncertainty and sit with it for a while. Too often, anger propels us
to take positions that we have not thought through carefully
enough or that we are not really ready to take. Nor does it
help that those around us may be full of advice and encouragement to act: "Leave that man, already!" "Tell your boss
that you won't do the assignment." "You just can't let him
treat you that way." "Tell her you won't be friends with her
anymore if she does that again." "Just tell him no."

Slow down! Our anger can be a powerful vehicle for
personal growth and change if it does nothing more than
help us recognize that we are not yet clear about something
and that it is our job to keep struggling with it. Let us look
at one woman's journey from an angry, blaming position to
a productive confronting of her own confusion.

6

UP AND DOWN
THE GENERATIONS

Katy and Her
Aging Father

Katy is a fifty-year-old homemaker whose youngest child has just left home for college. Her father is a seventy-two-year-old retired teacher who has been widowed for ten years and who is in moderately poor health. Katy called me at the Menninger Foundation because she had heard that I was an "anger expert." During our initial telephone conversation, she described a pattern that has been the source of her anger for almost a decade.

"My father has a big problem," she explained, with unveiled desperation in her voice. "He makes excessive demands on me, especially since he can't drive anymore because he lost some vision following a stroke. I'm supposed to take him shopping when he calls and drive him to his appointments. He asks me to do things for him in his apartment and then criticizes me for not doing them right. There are many things he could do for himself, but he acts like a big baby. Sometimes he calls me two or three times in one day. When I tell him no, he withdraws and makes me feel guilty. I'm really at the end of my rope."

When I met with Katy for the first time and requested clarification, I heard more of the same:

"What is your problem as you see it?"

KATY: "My problem is that my father doesn't realize I have my own life. He thinks my world should revolve around him. Since my mother's death, he uses me to fill in the empty space and take over."

"What, specifically, have you said to your father about the problem?"

KATY: " 'Father, you have to realize that I have my own life and that you are asking too much. I wish you would stop making me feel guilty when I don't come around. I think you need to get out and meet people and not just isolate yourself and rely on me.' "

"How does your father respond to this?"

KATY: "He gets upset and won't speak to me for a while. Or sometimes he starts talking about his poor health and he makes me feel so guilty that it's not worth it."

"What do you do then?"

KATY: "Nothing. Nothing works—that is why I'm here."

What was striking, and also quite typical, about Katy's brief synopsis was that everything she said was about her father:

"My father doesn't realize I have my own life."

"My father thinks my world should revolve around him."

"My father uses me."

"My father asks too much."

"My father makes me feel guilty."

"My father needs to get out and meet people."

Katy is doing what most of us do when we are angry. She is judging, blaming, criticizing, moralizing, preaching, instructing, interpreting, and psychoanalyzing. There is not one statement from Katy that is truly about her own self.

As you read ahead, keep in mind the lessons you have learned from the previous chapters. Katy's problem with her father has certain similarities to Maggie's problem with her mother. Struggle a bit with your own thoughts and reactions to the questions that follow before reading mine.

Is Katy's Father Wrong to Make Such Demands? I don't know. Who among us can say with certainty how many demands this particular seventy-two-year-old widowed father should rightfully make on his grown daughter? If we were to ask ten different people for their opinion, we might get ten different answers, depending on the respondent's age, religion, nationality, socioeconomic class, sibling position, and family background. If I were in Katy's shoes, I would probably also complain that my father was "too demanding." But that's because I'm me. Another person in the same spot might feel happy to be so needed.

If we are searching for the ultimate "truth" of the matter (How much should a parent ask? How much should a daughter give?), we may be failing to appreciate that there are multiple ways of perceiving the same situation and that people think, feel, and react differently. If I persist in repeating this point, it is because it is an extremely difficult concept to grasp, and hold on to, when we are angry. Conflicting wants and different perceptions of the world do not mean that one party is "right" and the other is "wrong."

Does Katy Have a Right to be Angry? Is Her Anger at Her Father Legitimate? Of course. As I stated earlier, feeling angry is neither right nor wrong, legitimate nor illegitimate. We have a right to everything we feel, and Katy's anger deserves her attention and respect. But Katy's right to be angry does not mean that her father is to blame. Rather, Katy's chronic anger and resentment is a signal that she needs to re-evaluate her participation in her interactions with her father and consider how she might move differently in this important relationship.

What's Wrong with Katy's Communications to Her Dad? For starters, Katy is not being particularly tactful or strategic. Few people are able to listen well when they are being criticized or told what's wrong with them. Unless Katy has a remarkably flexible father, her statements are likely to elicit further defensiveness on his part and make it less likely that she will be heard.

Second, Katy's communications convey that she is an expert on her father's experience. Katy diagnoses her father as a selfish, neurotic, and demanding man who is using his daughter to fill up the empty space left by his deceased wife. This psychological interpretation may or may not fit. There are countless other possible explanations for father's behavior, as well.

Diagnosing the other person is a favorite pastime for most of us when stress is high. Although it can reflect a wish to provide a truly helpful insight, more often it is a subtle form of blaming and one-upmanship. When we diagnose, we assume that we can know what another person _really_ thinks, feels, or wants, or how the other person _should_ think, feel, or behave. But we can't know these things for sure. It is difficult enough to know these things about our own selves.

Who Has the Problem? "My father has a big problem. He makes excessive demands on me." These statements— Katy's opening words to me on the phone—reflect her conviction that it is her *father* who has the problem. And yet, from Katy's description, her father is able to identify his wishes, state them clearly, and even get what he wants.

Katy has the problem. She has yet to find a way to identify and clarify her own limits with her father so that she is not left feeling bitter and resentful. It is Katy who is struggling and in pain. This is *her* problem.

To say that Katy has a problem, however, is not to imply that she is wrong or to blame or at fault. "Who has the problem?" is a question that has nothing to do with guilt or culpability. The one who has the problem is simply the party who is dissatisfied with or troubled by a particular situation.

What Is Katy's Problem? Katy's problem is that she has not sorted out some major questions in her own mind: "What is my responsibility for my own life, and what is my responsibility toward my father?" "What is being selfish, and what is being true to my own wants and priorities?" "What amount of help *can* I give to my father without feeling angry or resentful?" Not until she comes up with clear-cut answers to these difficult questions can she meet her father on a different plane.

Katy's problem is not that her father "makes" her feel guilty. Another person cannot "make" us feel guilty; they can only try. Katy's father will predictably give her a hard time if she shifts the old pattern, but she alone is responsible for her own feelings—guilt included.

Surely, there are no simple answers. What would *your* reaction be if Katy were to clarify new limits with her father? Would you view her as selfish or would you cheer her new claim to selfhood? Who knows? How many of us can distinguish with confidence where our responsibilities to others begin and end? How can women—trained from birth to define ourselves through our loving care of others—know with confidence when it is time to finally say "Enough!"?

"A woman's work is never done" was the credo that Katy had lived out with her children, and now that the youngest was leaving home, she was continuing the drama with her elderly father. Katy, I learned, had been "giving" for most of her life, as her mother and grandmother had before her. Deep down, she felt too scared and guilty to reveal that long-buried part of herself that wanted to put forth her own needs and begin to take. Katy had devoted herself so exclusively to the needs of others that she had betrayed, if not lost, her own self. She felt the rage of her buried self but hadn't yet been able to use it in order to make changes.

No matter how much we sympathize or identify with Katy's situation, it is her problem, nonetheless. This is not to imply that Katy is neurotic, misguided, or wrong. Nor is it to say that she is the "cause" of her dilemma. The rules and roles of our families and society make it especially difficult for women to define ourselves apart from the wishes and expectations of others—and negative reactions from others, when we begin to pay primary attention to the quality and direction of our own lives, may certainly invite us to become anxious and guilty.

If, however, we do not use our anger to define ourselves clearly in every important relationship we are in—and manage our feelings as they arise—no one else will assume this responsibility for us.

Harnessing Unclarity

Katy sought my help because she wanted to "do something" with her father and she wanted me to tell her what that something was. The fact of the matter was that Katy—like most women—had more than enough people telling her what to do. Her mother, by example, had taught her that selflessness, self-sacrifice, and service were a woman's calling, and now Katy's friends were telling her that self-assertion was the key to her liberation. "Don't say yes when you really mean no" was the most oft-repeated statement that Katy heard from her advisers, until she herself began to believe that her problem might be solved if she could only find the courage to mutter this unspeakable two-letter word.

What Katy really needed to do was to calm down and do nothing, at least for a while. It is not wise to make decisions or to attempt to change a relationship at a time when we are feeling angry and intense. Also, Katy has really not thought very much about her situation, because she is too busy reacting to it.

Katy would get off to a good start if she stopped blaming and diagnosing her father. She could begin to recognize that it is *her* job to separate herself a bit from his wishes and expectations in order to clarify her own values, to evaluate her own choices and priorities and to make decisions regarding what she will and will not do. Katy could also recognize that she is not yet clear about these things and does not know how to solve her problem. Acknowledging our unclarity is, in itself, a significant step.

What could Katy do next? What can any of us do when we feel angry in reaction to demands being placed upon us but see no new options for changing our behavior? Our anger signals a problem, but it provides us with no answers—not even a clue—as to how to solve it. Anger is simply something we feel—or allow ourselves to feel. At the same time it tells us that we need to slow down and think more clearly about the self, our anger can make clear thinking difficult indeed!

At this point, Katy's task is not to "do something" with her anger, although criticizing her father and inviting others to do the same may bring her short-term relief or at least a sense of moral superiority. In terms of lasting change, Katy's job is to strive to achieve a lower degree of emotional reactivity and a higher degree of self-clarity. How? Katy will become clearer about her convictions and options if she does the following: First, she can *share her problem* with other family members, including her father; second, she can *gather data* about how other relatives—especially the women in her family—have dealt with similar problems over the generations.

"Dad, I Have a Problem"

When Katy told her father a little about her problem, it was a high-anxiety moment and no less significant than Maggie's talk with her mother. By calmly sharing something about where she stood on an emotional issue in the family, Katy shifted the old rigid pattern in the relationship. The conversation went something like this:

"You know, Dad, I have a problem. I haven't figured

out how to balance the responsibility I feel toward you and the responsibility I feel toward myself. Last week when I took you shopping two times and also drove you to your doctor's appointment, I found myself feeling tense and uncomfortable, because I really wanted some of that time just for me. But when I say no and go about my own personal business, I end up feeling guilty—like I'm looking over my shoulder to see how you're doing."

"Well, if I'm that much of a burden, I can just stay away," father said coldly. He looked as if he had been physically struck.

Katy had prepared herself for her father's countermoves so that she could stand her ground when they came, without getting sucked into that intense field of emotional reactivity that characterized their relationship. "No, Dad," she replied, "I wouldn't want that. I'm not saying that *you* are burdening me. In fact, I would like to get a little better myself at asking people for help. What I'm talking about is *my* problem getting clear about what feels comfortable for me. I need to figure out how much I can do for you and when I need to say no and put myself first."

"Katy, you surprise me," said her father. "Your mother took care of both her parents when they were old and she never complained about it. Your mother would certainly not be very proud of you."

"I know what you mean, Dad." Katy refused to bite the bait and she continued to calmly address her own issue. "I was always impressed by Mom's willingness to take care of both her parents. It seemed to me that she had an amazing capacity to be giving, without feeling short-changed or resentful. But I'm not Mom. I'm different, and I really don't think I could do that. I guess I *am* more selfish than Mother was."

There was an awkward silence, which her father broke: "Well, Katy, is there something I'm supposed to do about this problem of yours?" The mixture of sarcasm and hurt in his voice couldn't be missed.

For a moment, Katy felt that old pressure to give her father advice and suggest ways that he could meet people and make use of the resources available to him. She knew from experience, however, that it didn't work. Instead, she stayed on course and continued to discuss her own problem:

"I wish someone else could solve my problem and make my decisions for me, but I know that's really my job." Katy became thoughtful. "Actually, Dad, it would be helpful to me, in my attempts to get clear about all this, if you could share some of your own experience with me. Have you ever struggled with anything like this? What was it like for you when your mother became ill and couldn't take care of herself anymore? Who in the family made the decision to put her in the nursing home, and what was your perspective on that?"

By directly addressing a family issue (in this case, "Who takes care of an elderly parent?") rather than angrily *reacting* to it, Katy detoxified the subject by getting it out on the table. As a result, the underground anxiety that surrounds unaddressed emotional issues will diminish and Katy will find that she is able to think more objectively about her situation. In addition, Katy is beginning to question her dad about his own experience with elderly parents. Learning how other family members have handled problems similar to our own, down through the generations, is one of the most effective routes to lowering reactivity and heightening self-clarity. In fact, *before* Katy could initiate this talk with her dad in so solid a fashion, she had to learn more about the legacy of caretaking in her family background.

LEARNING ABOUT OUR LEGACY

Which women in Katy's extended family have struggled with a similar problem and how have they attempted to solve it? How have other women in Katy's family—her sister, aunts, and grandmothers—balanced their responsibility to others with their responsibility to their selves? How successful have they been?

How did it happen that Katy's mother took on the sole responsibility of caring for her aging parents? What is the perspective of her mother's sister and brothers about how well this arrangement worked out?

How did decisions get made, down through the generations, about who took care of family members who were not able to care for themselves?

We are never the first in our family to wrestle with a problem, although it may feel that way. All of us inherit the unsolved problems of our past; and whatever we are struggling with has its legacy in the struggles of prior generations. *If we do not know about our own family history, we are more likely to repeat past patterns or mindlessly rebel against them, without much clarity about who we really are, how we are similar to and different from other family members, and how we might best proceed in our own life.*

Using our anger effectively requires first and foremost a clear "I," and women have been blocked from selfhood at every turn. We cannot hope to realize the self, however, in isolation from individuals on our family tree. No book—or psychotherapist, for that matter—can help us with this task if we stay cut off from our roots. Most of us react strongly to family members—especially our mothers—but we do not talk to them in depth and gather data about their experience. We may know virtually nothing about the forces that shaped our parents' lives as they shaped ours, or how our mothers and grandmothers dealt with problems similar to ours. When we do not know these things, we do not know the self. And without a clear self, rooted in our history, we will be prone to intense angry reactions in all sorts of situations, in response to which we will blame others, distance ourselves, passively comply, or otherwise spin our wheels.

And so, Katy had some "family work" to do. She contacted a wide representation of family members—especially the women—and learned firsthand about their experience and perspective as they grappled with issues not unlike her own. From living family members, she learned more about those who had died, including her mother. In so doing, Katy was able to see her problem with her father in its broader context.

Katy discovered that women in her family tended to fall into two opposite camps: those who, like her mother, made large personal sacrifices to care for aging parents and grandparents; and those who, like her mother's sister, Aunt Peggy, stuck their heads in the sand as aging family members became unable to care for themselves. Within these camps were several warring factions. Katy's mother, for example, did not speak to her sister for several years following their mother's death, because she felt that Peggy had not pitched in her share of the caretaking. From Peggy's perspective

Katy's mother had made unilateral and unwise decisions about their mother's care. Caring for elderly parents had been such a loaded issue in the previous generations that it was predictable that Katy would have a hard time finding a middle ground, and striking a comfortable balance between her responsibility for herself and her responsibility to her father.

As Katy connected to her family and gathered information, she felt calmer about her situation and was able to think about new options for herself with her father, where before she had been convinced that none were possible. There were no easy answers or painless solutions. Katy once summarized her dilemma this way: "No matter how long I'm in therapy, I'm still going to feel guilty if I say no to my father. But if I keep saying yes, I'm going to feel angry. So, if I'm going to change, I guess I will just have to learn to live with some guilt for a while." This is exactly what Katy did: She lived with some guilt, which did not prove fatal and which eventually subsided.

The specific changes that Katy made with her father may seem small and unimpressive to an outsider. She decided to have dinner with him twice rather than three times a week, and told him that she would shop for him on Saturday rather than on an "on-call" basis during the week. These were the only changes that she initiated, but she held to them and they made a big difference in her life. Soon thereafter, her father initiated a change of his own: He became good friends with an older woman in his neighborhood and they would talk for several hours each day. Katy felt reassured but also disquieted by this event. She began to realize how much her preoccupation with her father had organized her life and helped her to avoid confronting her isolation from her own peers. She also learned that she was far more skilled at giving help than asking for it.

The specifics of what Katy decided to do and not do for her father is the least important part of her story. Katy's solution would not necessarily be the right one for you or me. What is more significant is the work that she did in her own family which gave her a greater sense of connectedness to her roots and of her separateness and clarity as an individual. Now she could better use her anger as a springboard for *thinking* about her situation rather than remaining a victim of it. And as we will see, thinking clearly about the questions "What am I responsible for?" and "What am I *not* responsible for?" is a difficult challenge for all of us.

7

WHO'S RESPONSIBLE
FOR WHAT

The Trickiest
Anger Question

While attending a conference in New York one spring, I rode by bus to the Metropolitan Museum with two colleagues. I had lost my old familiarity with the city, and my companions, Celia and Janet, felt like foreigners in a strange land. Perhaps as a result of our "big-city" anxiety, we reminded the bus driver—once too often—to announce our stop. In a sudden and unexpected fury, he launched into a vitriolic attack that turned heads throughout the crowded bus. The three of us stood in stunned silence.

Later, over coffee, we shared our personal reactions to this incident. Celia felt mildly depressed. She was reminded of her abusive ex-husband and this particular week was the anniversary of their divorce. Janet reacted with anger, which seemed to dissipate as she drummed up clever retorts to the driver's outburst and hilarious revenge fantasies. My own reaction was nostalgia. I had been feeling homesick for New York and almost welcomed the contrast to the midwestern politeness to which I had become accustomed. It was a New

York City "happening" that I could take back to Topeka, Kansas.

Suppose we reflect briefly on this incident. We might all agree that the bus driver behaved badly. But is he also responsible for the reactions of three women? Did he *cause* Celia's depression and Janet's anger? Did he *make* me feel nostalgic for my past? And if one of us had reacted to this man's surliness by jumping off the Brooklyn Bridge that night, should he be held accountable for a death? Or, viewed from another perspective, were *we* responsible for his outburst to begin with?

It is tempting to view human transactions in simple cause-and-effect terms. If we are angry, someone else *caused* it. Or, if we are the target of someone else's anger, we must be to *blame;* or, alternately—if we are convinced of our innocence—we may conclude that the other person has no *right* to feel angry. The more our relationships in our first family are fused (meaning the togetherness force is so powerful that there is a loss of the separate "I's" within the "we"), the more we learn to take responsibility for other people's feelings and reactions and blame them for our own. ("You always make Mom feel guilty." "You give Dad headaches." "She caused her husband to drink.") Likewise, family members assume responsibility for *causing* other people's thoughts, feelings, and behavior.

Human relationships, however, don't work that way— or at least not very well. We begin to use our anger as a vehicle for change when we are able to share our reactions without holding the other person responsible for causing our feelings, and without blaming ourselves for the reactions that other people have in response to our choices and actions.

We *are* responsible for our own behavior. But we are *not* responsible for other people's reactions; nor are they responsible for ours. Women often learn to reverse this order of things: *We put our energy into taking responsibility for other people's feelings, thoughts, and behavior and hand over to others responsibility for our own.* When this happens, it becomes difficult, if not impossible, for the old rules of a relationship to change.

To illustrate the point, let's return to Katy's problem with her widowed father, whom she initially described as excessively demanding and guilt-inducing. If Katy perceives her father as unilaterally causing her anger and/or guilt, she is at a dead end. She will feel helpless and powerless because she cannot change him. Similarly, if Katy takes responsibility for causing her father's feelings and reactions, she is also stuck. Why? Because if Katy does make a change in the status quo, her father will become emotionally reactive to her new behavior. If Katy then feels responsible for causing his reactions, she may reinstate the old pattern in order to protect her father (and herself) from uncomfortable feelings and to safeguard the predictable sameness of the relationship. ("My father got so angry and crazy when I said no that there was just nothing I could do.") The situation is then defined as hopeless.

Why is the question "Who is responsible for what?" such a puzzle for women? Women in particular have been discouraged from taking responsibility for solving our own problems, determining our own choices, and taking control of the quality and direction of our own lives. As we learn to relinquish responsibility for the self, we are prone to blame others for failing to fill up our emptiness or provide for our happiness—which is not their job. At the same time, however, we may feel responsible for just about everything that goes on around us. We are quick to be blamed for other people's problems and pain and quick to accept the verdict of guilty. We also, in the process, develop the belief that we *can* avert problems if only we try hard enough. Indeed, guilt and self-blame are a "woman's problem" of epidemic proportion. A colleague tells the story of pausing on a ski slope to admire the view, only to be knocked down by a careless skier who apparently did not notice her. "I'm s-o-r-r-y," she reflexively yelled after him from her prone position as he whizzed on by.

In this chapter we will see how confusion about "Who is responsible for what?" is one source of nonproductive self-blaming and other-blaming, as well as a roadblock to changing our situation. How can we learn to take *more* responsibility for the self and *less* for the thoughts, feelings, and behavior of others? At this point, you should be clearer on the subject than when you started out, but let's continue to try our hand at sorting out the elements of this perplexing question. Remember—assuming responsibility for the self means not only clarifying the "I" but also observing and changing our part in the patterns that keep us stuck. In this chapter we will be looking carefully at the *overfunctioning-underfunctioning patterns* in which we all participate.

A CRISIS AT MIDNIGHT

Jane and Stephanie have lived together for eight years and have raised a German shepherd who is a much-loved member of their household. One evening the dog woke them in the middle of the night and was obviously quite ill. Stephanie thought that the situation was serious enough to warrant an immediate call to the vet. Jane insisted that it could wait till morning. She accused Stephanie of being excessively worried and overreactive.

When they awoke the next morning, their dog's condition had worsened. When the veterinarian examined him, she said, "You should have called me immediately. Your dog could have died." Stephanie was furious at Jane. "If anything had happened," she said, "*you* would have been to blame!"

What is your perspective on this situation?

How would you react if you were in Stephanie's shoes at this point?

How do you view the responsibility of each party in contributing to Stephanie's anger?

We may empathize with Stephanie's anger, but she is nonetheless confused about who is responsible for what. Let's analyze the situation in more detail.

It is Jane's responsibility to clarify her beliefs and take action in accord with them. She did this. It was her opinion that the dog did not need immediate medical attention and so she did not call the doctor. Stephanie, too, is responsible for clarifying *her* beliefs and acting upon them. She did *not* do this. She was worried that the dog might need immediate attention and still she did not call the vet.

I am not suggesting that Stephanie should not feel angry with Jane. If she is angry, she is angry. She may be angry that Jane put down her fears, minimized her concerns, disqualified her perception of reality, or acted like a know-it-all. Nonetheless, it is Stephanie, not Jane, who has the ultimate responsibility for what Stephanie decides to do or not to do.

"But You Don't Know Jane!"

"The reason I didn't call," Stephanie explained later, "is that Jane would never have let me hear the end of it if I was wrong. If I had woken the vet up in the middle of the night for nothing, Jane would have been on my case for weeks and she'd have one more reason to label me a neurotic worrier. I love Jane, but you don't know how difficult she can be! She is so sure of herself that it makes me question my own opinions." In this formulation, Stephanie continues to blame Jane for her (Stephanie's) behavior.

Of course, if Stephanie does begin to assert her own self, Jane may have an intense reaction—especially if Jane has operated as the dominant partner whenever decisions had to be made. But if Stephanie can stick to her position without emotionally distancing or escalating tensions further, chances are that over time Jane will manage her own feelings and reactions just fine.

What are the steps we can take to translate our anger into a clear sense of personal responsibility that will result in more functional relationships with others? Some steps for Stephanie are: observation, clarifying the pattern, and gathering data.

OBSERVATION

Imagine that you are in Stephanie's shoes and feeling angry—not just about the dog incident but also about the relationship pattern that this incident brought to light. What might be your next step?

The first step in the direction of gaining greater clarity about who is responsible for what is to begin to *carefully observe* the sequences of interaction that lead up to our feeling angry or emotionally intense. For example, Stephanie might observe that the pattern around decision-making often goes like this:

A situation occurs (in this case, a sick dog) that requires a decision. Stephanie tends to respond first by voicing a rather tentative opinion. Jane then states her own opinion, which may be different, in a supremely confident manner. Stephanie then begins to doubt her initial opinion, or simply concludes that "it's not worth the fight." In either case, she defers to Jane. Often this pattern works fine for both of them and things remain calm. But when anxiety and stress are high (as in the present example), Stephanie becomes angry with Jane if the outcome of Jane's decision-making is not to her liking. Stephanie then either withdraws from Jane or criticizes her decision. If she does the latter, a fight ensues, and by the next day things are usually calm again.

CLARIFYING THE PATTERN

Although she might define it differently, Stephanie is beginning to identify an overfunctioning-underfunctioning pattern around decision-making. The more Jane *overfunctions* (jumps in to make decisions for the two of them; fails to express any doubt or insecurity about her own judgment; behaves as if she does not benefit from Stephanie's help and advice), the more Stephanie *underfunctions* (spaces out or does nothing when a decision is to be made; relies on Jane to take over; feels lazy or less competent to make important decisions). And the more Stephanie *underfunctions*, the more Jane will *overfunction*. Overfunctioners and underfunctioners reinforce each other's behavior in a circular fashion.

Approaching a relationship pattern in this way—gathering the objective data about who does what, when, and in what order—is difficult enough when things are calm. It is next to impossible if we are locked into emotionally intense and blaming behavior. We have seen how women learn to be the emotional reactors in our relationships, especially when stress hits, so we may need to make a conscious effort to become less reactive in order to focus our attention on the task of getting the facts.

GATHERING DATA

Stephanie will also benefit from gathering some data about how this pattern of relating to Jane fits with her own family tradition over the generations. For example, how did Stephanie's parents, and their parents before them, negotiate issues of decision-making? In Stephanie's extended family, which relationships were characterized by a balance of power and which marriages had one dominant (overfunctioning) partner who was viewed as having the corner on competence? How is Stephanie's relationship with Jane similar to and different from her parents' relationship with regard to the sharing of decision-making power? What other women in Stephanie's family have struggled to shift away from the underfunctioning position and how successful were they? As we saw with Katy, our current relationship struggles are part of a legacy that began long before our birth. A familiarity with this legacy helps us gain objectivity when evaluating our behavior in relationships.

Birth order is another factor that strongly influences our way of negotiating relationships. In Stephanie and Jane's case, for example, their pattern around decision-making fits their sibling positions. Jane is the older of two sisters. It is characteristic of one in this sibling position to be a natural leader and to believe, in one's heart of hearts, that one truly knows best, not only for oneself, but for the other person as well. Stephanie is the younger of the two sisters in her family, and, in the manner of one in that position, is often comfortable letting other people do things for her. Although she may compete fiercely with the "leader," she may also shun leadership should it be offered her. Simply being aware that one's sibling position within the family affects one's approach to life can be extremely helpful. If Stephanie finds herself having a hard time taking charge of things, and Jane an equally hard time *not* taking charge, they will both be able to deal with their situation with more humor and less self-criticism if they can appreciate the fact that they are behaving much the way people in their sibling positions behave under stress.

SO WHO HAS THE PROBLEM?

Let us suppose that Stephanie has taken the following steps since the dog incident: First, she has let go of her blaming position ("If anything had happened, *you* would have been to blame!") and has begun to *think* about, rather than simply react to, the problem. Second, she has pretty clearly figured out who does what, when, and in what order; when stress hits, Stephanie underfunctions and Jane overfunctions. Third, Stephanie has thought about how this pattern fits with the traditions in her own family. Finally, she has concluded that she is in a de-selfed position and that her anger is a signal that she would like to achieve more balance in her relationship with Jane when it comes to decision-making.

The following dialogues reflect two modes of using our anger: The first assumes that Jane has the problem and it is her responsibility to take care of it. The second assumes that

Stephanie has the problem and it is her responsibility to take care of it.

DIALOGUE 1

"Jane, you are so damned sure of yourself. You're impossible to argue with because you're always right and you don't really listen to my opinions in any open way. You come on so strong that no one can argue with you. I'm really fed up with your know-it-all attitude. When I give my opinion, you pronounce it true or not true, like you're God or something. You make me feel totally insecure about my own thinking. And you always take over and manipulate things to get your way."

DIALOGUE 2

"You know, Jane, I've been thinking about the problem that I have in our relationship. I think it has to do with how difficult it is for me to make decisions and take charge of things. I didn't call the vet the other night because when you expressed such confidence in your opinion, I began to doubt my own. And when you were critical of my opinion and put me down for being so worried—which I don't like—I reacted by being even more ready to back down. I'm aware that I do this a lot. And I'm planning to work harder to make my own decisions and stand behind them. I'm sure I'll make mistakes and our relationship might be more tense for a while—but I'm just not satisfied with things as they are. However, I'm also aware that the women in my family haven't done too well making their own decisions—so it may not be easy for me to be a pioneer in this way."

What about dialogue 1? Some relationships thrive on

tough confrontation, and feedback of this sort and fighting it out may be viewed by both partners as a valuable and spicy aspect of the relationship. For all we know, Jane might respond to dialogue 1 by becoming thoughtful and saying, "You know, I've been told that before by other people in my life. I think you have something there. I'm sorry for coming on so strong and I'll try to watch it."

This dialogue does, however, reflect Stephanie's confusion about the matter of individual responsibility. Can you spot the problem? She holds Jane responsible for Jane's behavior (putting Stephanie down), which is fair enough; but she also holds Jane responsible for Stephanie's behavior (feeling insecure and manipulated and failing to stand firmly behind her own opinion), which is not fair at all. Blaming of this sort blurs the boundaries between self and other in a close relationship.

What about dialogue 2? Here, Stephanie shares something about herself and does not assume to be an expert on Jane. She talks about her own dilemma in the relationship and takes responsibility for her own part.cipation in the pattern. While dialogue 1 might lead to a further escalation of an already stressful situation, dialogue 2 would probably calm things down a bit and foster greater objectivity on both women's parts.

Which dialogue better suits your personal style? For me, it depends on the relationship. With my husband, Steve, I sometimes dissipate tension by fighting dialogue-1 style, although with less frequency and intensity as I get older. At work, however, and during visits from long-distance friends and family, I end up feeling much better if I communicate in dialogue-2 style, and I find that these relationships do better, too. It all depends on what the circumstances are, what your goals are, and what in the past has left you feeling better or worse in the long run.

Of course, what is most important is not what Stephanie says to Jane but what she does. Next time around, perhaps Stephanie will listen to Jane and consider her perspective but then take responsibility to make her own reasoned decision about what she will and won't do. Stephanie's communication style will make little difference if she does not modify her own underfunctioning position.

As we learn to identify relationship patterns, we are faced with a peculiar paradox: On the one hand, our job is to learn to take responsibility for our thoughts, feelings, and behavior and to recognize that other people are responsible for their own. Yet, at the same time, how we react with others has a great deal to do with how they react with us. We cannot *not* influence a relationship pattern. Once a relationship is locked into a circular pattern, the whole cycle will change when one person takes the responsibility for changing her or his own part in the sequence.

Assuming this responsibility does not mean we take a self-blaming or self-deprecating position. Learning to observe and change our behavior is a self-loving process that can't take place in an atmosphere of self-criticism or self-blame. Such attitudes frequently undermine, rather than enhance, our ability to observe relationship patterns. They may even be part of the game we learn to play in which the unconscious goal is to safeguard relationships by being one down in order to help the other person feel one up.

In contrast, it is a position of dignity and strength that allows us to say to ourselves or others, "You know, I observe that this is what I am doing in this relationship and I am now going to work to change it." Such owning of responsibility does not let the other person off the hook. To the contrary, we have seen how it brings our "separateness" into bold relief and confronts others with the fact that we alone bear the ultimate responsibility for defining our selves and the terms of our own lives. It respectfully allows others to do the same.

WHO'S DOING THE HOUSEWORK?

After countless housework battles with her husband, Lisa decided to cease and desist from the old fights and begin to clarify her own problem. She chose a moment when things were relatively calm and close between them and said, "Rich, I'm having a problem with the amount of housework I do. When I take on more than half the responsibility for cooking and cleaning, I end up feeling resentful, because the way I see it, I'm pulling more than my fair share of the load. I'm exhausted as well. I guess my biggest problem is that I am tired too much of the time and I need to find a way to conserve my energy and have more time for myself." Then Lisa told Rich specifically what she would like him to do in order to help out.

Lisa did not criticize her husband or instruct him on how a good man behaves; rather, she was sharing her feelings about a situation that had become increasingly problematic for her. When Rich said, "Well, other women I know seem to manage just fine," Lisa said lightly, "Well, I'm not other women. I'm me."

Several months later, Rich was doing nothing more than taking the garbage out and tending to yard work and Lisa was still angry. As she and I talked, however, I became aware that she had made no change in her own behavior. As usual, she was entertaining Rich's colleagues, doing his laundry, cooking dinner, washing the dishes, even vacuuming his study. Lisa's words were saying, "I'm tired and resentful and I need to do something about it." Her actions, however, were maintaining the status quo. She was not taking responsibility for doing something about her problem.

But why should she? Isn't Rich the one who should change his behavior? Is it not his responsibility to behave fairly and considerately toward his wife? Lisa is forever trying to initiate change in this relationship—so, isn't it Rich's turn?

You and I may think so, but that's beside the point. Rich does not have a problem with the current situation. He is satisfied with things as they are and he is not interested in making a change. If Lisa does not proceed to take care of what is *her* problem, no one else will do it for her, her husband included.

When the day came that Lisa could no longer stand her predicament, she began to make her actions congruent with her words. First, Lisa figured out a plan. She made a list of tasks that she would continue to do (for example, a clean living room and kitchen were extremely important to her, so she would not let things pile up here) and a list of those that she would no longer do. For these, she hoped that Rich would fill in, but if not, they would just live without their being done. Then she shared the plan with Rich and put it into force.

Lisa stood behind her position as Rich tested her out for two months by becoming even more of a slob than usual. Lisa continued to do more of the housework because a clean house was more important to her than it was to Rich. She found other ways, however, to save her time and energy.

For three nights a week she made sandwiches for her and the kids for dinner and let Rich prepare his own meals when he came home from work. If Rich invited his friends or colleagues to dinner, she did not shop or cook for the event, although she was glad to help out. Lisa carefully sorted out where she wanted to put her time and energy and where she could conserve it.

Lisa made these changes out of a sense of responsibility for herself—not as a move against Rich. If she had gone "on strike," or this was no more than a plot to shape Rich up or to get back at him, the probable outcome for this couple might well have been an escalation of their difficulties.

As a postscript, I might add that as Rich made some changes of his own, Lisa, in reaction, made some counter-moves. If you recall, "Please change!" and "Change back!" are the mixed messages that we often give each other. When Rich took the initiative to do housework, Lisa was right there to offer unsolicited advice or to criticize him for not being thorough enough. To ask a person to do more housework (or parenting) and then say "Do it the way I would do it" or "Do it the way I want you to" is a *move that blocks change*. If Lisa is truly ready to have Rich more involved with the housework (which means that she is willing to give up some control in this area), she must also be ready to *let Rich do it his own way*. If she wants him to stop underfunctioning in this area, she must be willing to stop overfunctioning. Obviously, Rich may never clean house up to her standards, which are likely to be different from his. However, if Lisa can credit his attempts and truly stay out (unless he asks for her advice or feedback), his housekeeping skills will get better in time.

Lisa had an additional problem as Rich began to change:

She not only wanted him to do more of the housework; she wanted him to *want* to. "He did the dishes last night," she moaned, "but he sulked and pouted for the rest of the evening. It's just not worth it." Again, we see Lisa's discomfort with change. Sulking and pouting is *Rich's* problem, and it is not Lisa's business or responsibility to fix or take away his feelings. Although no one has died from sulking yet, women, the emotional rescuers of the world, can have a terribly difficult time allowing others just to sit with their feelings and learn to handle them. If Lisa can avoid becoming distant and critical, and if she can allow Rich the space to sulk as he pleases without reacting to it, his sulking will eventually subside. But when she says "It's just not worth it," this *is* Lisa's problem and reflects her own mixed feelings about changing a long-standing relationship pattern.

Why should it be easy for Lisa to relinquish control in an area where female authority and competence have gone unquestioned generation after generation? When Lisa does housework, she is linked to her mother, to her grandmothers, and to all the women who have come before. It is part of her heritage and tradition, to say nothing of the fact that homemaking is important and valuable work—no matter how little recognition it gets. Sure, housework can be tedious and daily living easier when it is shared, but it is understandable that Lisa may have some complicated feelings about it all. And perhaps Lisa has few other areas where she, rather than Rich, can assume the role of the competent expert.

One last question: If Lisa is serious about change, why not a good let-it-all-hang-out fight? Can't Lisa let Rich know by the volume of her voice that she really means business? *Nothing is wrong with fighting if it leaves Lisa feeling better and if it is part of a process by which Lisa gains a greater clarity that she will not proceed with things as usual.* In ongoing battles of this sort, the single most important factor is not whether we fight or not, or whether our voice is raised or calm; it is the growing inner conviction that we can no longer continue to overfunction (in Lisa's case, on the domestic scene), for our own sake.

Emotional Overfunctioning— More "Women's Work"

Earlier we noted the ways in which de-selfing and *under-functioning* are prescribed for women—and so they are. Thus, when we have our own area of *overfunctioning*, we may do it with a vengeance while complaining all the way, as Lisa did with housework. In addition to picking up someone else's socks, how else are we likely to overfunction?

Often in relationships, women overfunction by assuming a "rescuing" or "fix-it" position. We behave as if it is our responsibility to shape up other people or solve their problems, and further, that it is in our power to do so. We may become reactive to every move that a person makes or fails to make, our emotions ranging from annoyance to intense anger or despair. And when we realize that our attempts to be helpful are not working, do we stop and do something different? Of course not! As we saw with Sandra and Larry (Chapter 3), we may redouble our unsuccessful efforts, only to become angrier and angrier at that underfunctioning individual who is not shaping up.

What a difficult time we may have maintaining the degree of separateness that allows others the space to manage their own pain and solve their own problems! Men also have this difficulty balancing the forces of separateness and togetherness; however, they tend to handle anxiety by emotional distancing and disengaging (thus, sacrificing the "we" for the "I"), whereas women more frequently handle anxiety by fusion and emotional overfunctioning (thus, sacrificing the "I" for the "we"). The sex-role division for these two unhappy and out-of-balance alternatives is hardly surprising. Our society undervalues the importance of close relationships for men and fosters their emotional isolation and disconnectedness. Women, on the other hand, receive an opposite message that encourages us to be excessively focused on, and fused with, the problems of others, rather than putting our primary "worry energy" into our own problems. *When we do not put our primary emotional energy into solving our own problems, we take on other people's problems as our own.*

But what is wrong with taking responsibility for others? In some respects, nothing. For generations, women have gained both identity and esteem from our deep investment in protecting, helping, nurturing, and comforting others. Surely, connectedness to others, empathy and loving regard for our fellow human beings, and investment in facilitating the growth of the young are virtues of the highest order for both women and men. The problem arises when we are excessively reactive to other people's problems, when we assume responsibility for things that we are not responsible for, and when we attempt to control things that are not in our control. When we overfunction for another individual, we end up very angry, and in the process, we facilitate the growth of no one.

The saga of overfunctioning will come more clearly to light as we unravel the story of Lois and her brother. As you read, keep in mind that it could as easily be Lois and her son, her grandfather, her mother-in-law, her employee, or her friend.

"MY BROTHER IS A MESS!"

"I don't mean to sound unsympathetic or callous," explained Lois, who sounded as if she was about to disown her younger brother, Brian. "Obviously, I'm very concerned about Brian because he's so screwed up. But I also find myself angry with him. Two things that he does irritate the hell out of me: First, he always calls in the middle of some kind of crisis and wants to borrow some money and ask for advice. Then he spends the money—which he never pays back—and ignores the advice. I've referred him to two therapists, but he didn't stick with it. I've suggested books for him to read to get his life together. I've talked on the phone with him when he calls me—collect, of course—and I tell him what he can do to get his act together. Brian listens and then he doesn't do it. I've tried some tough confrontation and that doesn't work, either. I'm feeling drained and I'm feeling angry. Yet, he's my brother and I can't turn him away. He's alienated my parents and he has nowhere else to go."

What is the pattern of interaction between Lois and her brother? Brian calls, saying "Help!" Lois jumps in to help. Brian then continues his old ways, and sooner or later he calls again with a new crisis. Lois takes either a tough or a sympathetic approach, but in either case she continues to tell her little brother (who is twenty-four years old) how to shape up. Brian does not shape up. Lois gets angry and the cycle continues.

So, who is to blame for this merry-go-round? Hopefully, by now you are no longer thinking in these terms. Relationships are circular (A and B are mutually reinforcing) rather than linear (A causes B or B causes A). *Once a pattern is established in a relationship, it is perpetuated by both parties.*

What is Lois's part in keeping the circular dance going? The more she overfunctions, the more Brian will underfunction—which means that the more Lois is helpful, the more Brian will need her help. The more Lois fails to express her own doubts, vulnerability, or incompetence to Brian, the more Brian will express enough for both of them. The more emotional Lois gets about Brian's problems, the more he won't care enough about himself. Lois's big-sisterly sense of responsibility may have many positive aspects. Nonetheless, she is functioning at the expense of her brother's competence.

Does this mean that Lois is responsible for her brother's problems? Not at all. She does not *make* Brian incompetent to manage his life any more than Brian *makes* Lois rescue him. Lois's role as rescuer and Brian's as rescuee have their roots in family patterns that can be traced back for generations. They are each responsible for their own behavior, and Lois's behavior is fifty percent of the problem she complains of. What are your thoughts about the specific steps Lois might take to change it?

What about sharing her problem with Brian in a nonblaming way? Lois could approach him when things are calm in their relationship and say, "When you call me to ask for money and advice, my initial reaction is to give it. But after I give it and I see that it hasn't really helped, I start to feel resentful. Maybe it's partly from my own wish to be helpful that I end up feeling frustrated. But I don't want things to continue this way. Please don't ask me to lend you money unless you can pay it back. And please don't ask me for advice if you're just going to do your own thing anyway."

It won't work—or at least it won't change the pattern.

Communication of this sort is preferable to blaming Brian ("Brian, you're an exploitative, irresponsible, manipulative psychopath") or interpreting his motives ("I think you are using me"). Nonetheless, if Lois wishes to change this over-functioning-underfunctioning pattern, she cannot do so simply by expressing her feelings or asking Brian to change. *She will have to stop overfunctioning.* What specifically does this mean?

Learning How Not to Be Helpful

If Lois wants to change the old pattern with Brian, she can put the brakes on being helpful. Sound simple? For those of us who believe it is our sacred calling to save other people and shape them up, the hardest thing in the world is to *stop* trying to be helpful.

How does one go about not trying to be helpful? How does one stop rescuing another family member? Here's an example:

The next time Brian calls Lois in distress, Lois can listen sympathetically and ask him questions about his situation. And she can say in a low-keyed way, "It sounds like you're really having a hard time, Brian. I'm sorry to hear that."

If Brian asks her for money, she can say, "I've decided not to lend you any more money, Brian. There are a bunch of things that I'm saving for and I've decided that's my first priority—you're on your own, kid." If Lois can do this with warmth and humor, all the better. For example, if Brian says accusingly, "That's selfish," Lois might say, "You're probably right. I think I am getting more selfish in my old age."

If Brian courts her advice, Lois can bite her tongue and say, "Well, I really just don't know," or, "I wish I could be helpful, but you know, Brian, I just don't know what to say."

Then Lois might proceed to share a little bit about what she is currently struggling with and perhaps ask Brian if he has any thoughts about *her* dilemma. Another thing Lois can do is to express confidence in Brian's ability to find his own solutions: "I know you've been struggling for a long time to get on top of things, but I have faith that you'll eventually work it out. I think you're a really bright guy."

Learning how not to be helpful requires a certain attitude toward relationships and an ability to strike the right balance between the forces of separateness and togetherness. If Lois's tone is, "Don't try to involve *me*, it's not *my* problem," the old pattern won't change. This is a reactive and distancing position. Similarly, if Lois says, "Well, I'm not going to give you any advice or money from now on because it's not good for *you*, Brian," she is simply doing another variation of her therapeutic "I-really-know-what's-best-for-you" attitude. Learning how *not* to be helpful requires that we begin to acknowledge that we do not have the answers or solutions to other people's problems. In fact, we don't even have the answers to all of our own.

What's Wrong with Advice-Giving?

Does this mean that Lois should never, ever offer Brian advice for as long as they both shall live? Down the road a bit, as the pattern starts to shift, Lois might give Brian advice *if* he asks for it and *if* she observes that it's useful. But there is advice-giving—and then there is advice-giving!

There is nothing wrong with giving another person advice ("This is what I think . . ." or, "In my experience, this has worked for me") as long as we recognize that we are stating an opinion that may or may not fit for the other person. We start to overfunction, however, when we assume that we know what's best for the other person and we want them to do it our way. If Lois feels angry when Brian does not follow her advice, that's a good indication that she should not be giving it.

It is also the case that those closest to us may have the greatest difficulty considering our advice if we come across as though we have the final word on their lives. Lois's typical style, for example, is to lecture Brian about the importance of his getting professional help and then to get angry at him for not following through. Brian would have a better opportunity to evaluate this option if Lois were to say (and only if asked), "Well, therapy has been pretty helpful to me in my own life, so I'm all for it. But not everyone is alike and you may be more of a do-it-yourselfer. What do you think?" Giving advice in this way is not just a strategic move; it is a mature approach that takes into account the separateness and "otherness" of her brother. Further, it acknowledges that people are different and that we all have the ability to become the best experts on our own selves.

Hanging In

As we saw with Maggie and her mother, there is hardly anything more important than emotionally hanging in— especially when we are shifting a pattern. Lois's task is to show her concern for Brian at the same time that she stops trying to help him solve his problems. How can she do this?

Lois can call Brian while he's having a hard time simply to touch base with him. She might say, "I know I'm not much help to you at this time, but I just wanted to hear how you're doing and let you know that I care about you." She might increase her contact with Brian and invite him to have dinner with her family. *Stepping back and allowing the other*

_person to struggle with his or her own problems is not the
same as emotional withdrawal._ Lois can stop trying to bail
Brian out, yet still express her support and interest as he
goes through a difficult time.

Maintaining emotional contact is never easy at this point
in a changing relationship. Our natural tendency may be
either to fight or to emotionally distance ourselves because
we are uncertain about our position and how to maintain it
in the face of pressures to do otherwise, a big part of which
is our own anxiety about really changing. Hanging in requires
us to move against enormous internal resistance, which is
most often experienced as anger ("Why should I get in touch
with him when he's acting this way?") or inertia ("I just
don't feel like taking the initiative").

Sharing Our Underfunctioning Side

In therapy sessions, Lois discussed her problems and pain
with me, but within her own family, and especially with
Brian, she was always fine and didn't need anything from
anybody. Like all good overfunctioners, Lois was convinced
that sharing her struggles and vulnerability with Brian was
absolutely out of the question. ("I would never tell Brian that
I was depressed; I have absolutely no desire to do so and he
has more than enough problems of his own." "Brian can't
deal with my feelings." "Why burden him; there is no way
he can be helpful to me.") The relationship between Lois and
Brian was extremely polarized, with Brian expressing only
his weakness and Lois only her competence.

If Lois wants to shift the old pattern, she can present a
more balanced picture of herself and begin to share a bit
about her own travails with Brian. For example, when Brian
calls to talk about his recent crises, Lois can say, "Brian, I

wish I could be more useful, but I'm no good for much of anything right now. In fact, I've been feeling lousy all day. I'm sorry you're feeling bad, but I just don't have much energy to give to anyone else. Part of the problem is that I've been feeling dissatisfied with my job for a long time, but today it really came to a head and I got real down in the dumps." If we are dealing with depressed or underfunctioning individuals, the least helpful thing we can do is to keep focusing on *their* problems and trying to be helpful. *The most helpful thing we can do is begin to share part of our own underfunctioning side.*

Ah, Yes, Countermoves!

Finally, Lois must be prepared to deal with Brian's countermoves. As sure as the sun rises in the morning, Brian will up the ante and attempt to reinstate the old pattern. If he has been requesting money to help pay his electric bills, his next request is bound to find him starving to death or about to be thrown in jail. This is the point at which we are truly put to the test. We either give ourselves an excuse to go back to our old ways and blame the other party ("Well, I couldn't let my own brother die in the streets, could I?"), or we sit with some anxiety and guilt and maintain our new position. If Lois can calmly continue not to rescue Brian or attempt to solve his problems—while offering him emotional support and contact—his countermoves are likely to decrease rather dramatically. They will pop up only periodically as he tests out the waters of their relationship over time.

What light does Lois's story shed on the question we started out with: "Who is responsible for what?" It provides us with a good example of how we may be too responsible for another person and, at the same time, not responsible enough for our own behavior. Lois is feeling angry because she assumes too much responsibility for her brother's problems; she advises, rescues, and bails Brian out. She has difficulty simply being there and letting him struggle on his own. At the same time, however, Lois does not assume enough responsibility for examining how her own behavior contributes to the pattern she's so eager to change. She is stuck in a position that blocks her from reflecting upon her situation and figuring out how she can take a new stance that will free her from the old rules and roles.

While it is hard to change in the short run, there are long-term costs of maintaining the status quo. Most obvious are the costs for Brian. Lois is a devoted big sister, but, by persisting in her unsuccessful attempts to advise and rescue her brother and failing to show him her own vulnerable side, she is doing the least helpful things that one can do with an underfunctioning individual. Less obvious but no less important is the price that Lois pays personally for the position she holds in this relationship, as evidenced by her chronic anger and high level of stress. When we overfunction, we may have a difficult time allowing others to take over and care for us, so that we can just relax or have the luxury of falling apart for a little while. Lois, the caretaker and helper for others, has lost sight of her own needs and challenges of continued growth, which she can sweep under the rug because she "needs to care for her brother." By continuing to feel responsible for the other party, Lois ends up underfunctioning for her own self.

ANGER AT KIDS

Self-blaming and child-blaming remain an occupational hazard for many mothers today. "What's wrong with me?" and/or "What's wrong with this child?" are the two questions mothers learn to ask themselves as they are handed over the primary responsibility for all family problems. We have fostered in mothers the omnipotent fantasy that their child's behavior—their very "being"—is mother's doing: If the child performs well, she is considered a "good mother"; if poorly, a "bad mother," who caused the problem. It is as if the mother *is* the child's environment. Until recently, father, the family, the society in which the family is embedded—all these did not *really* count.

As mothers, we are led to believe that we *can,* and *should,* control things that are not realistically within our control. Many of us do feel an excessive need to control our children's behavior, to prove to ourselves, to our own mothers, and to the world that we are good mothers. However, the mother who is dominated by anger because she feels helpless to control her child is often caught in that paradox that underlies our difficulties with this emotion. We may view it as our responsibility to control something that is not in fact within our control and yet fail to exercise the power and authority that we *do* have over our own behavior. Mothers cannot *make* children think, feel, or be a certain way, but we can be firm, consistent, and clear about what *behavior* we will and will not tolerate, and what the consequences are for misbehavior. We can also change our part in patterns that keep family members stuck. At the same time we are doomed to failure with any self-help venture if we view the problem as existing within ourselves—or within the child or the child's father, for that matter. There is never one villain in family life, although it may appear that way on the surface.

Angry power struggles with kids often boil down to this: We may *overfunction,* or move in too much, when it comes to their thoughts and feelings. At the same time, we may *underfunction* when it comes to clarifying our own position and setting rules about behavior. Here is a typical example:

CLAUDIA: A FOUR-YEAR-OLD DICTATOR

Alicia, who had been divorced for several months, was starting to date a man named Carlos. "I like him, but my daughter doesn't," Alicia explained. "Whenever Carlos and I are about to leave the house together, Claudia, who's four, begins to sob mournfully as if her little heart is breaking. Perhaps it has to do with her loyalty to her father, but she just doesn't like Carlos and she doesn't like me to be alone with him. She treats him rudely and refuses to speak to him. Sometimes she has a full-blown temper tantrum when the two of us are about to walk out the door. I feel such rage at her that I can't even be sympathetic."

"And what do you do when Claudia does these things?" I inquired.

"When I'm feeling calm, I try to *reason* with her," explained Alicia. "I let her know that I need to go out and that there is no reason for her to be upset about it. I tell her that soon she will get used to my going out and then it won't bother her. I explain to her that Carlos is a very nice man and that if only she would make the effort, she would like him."

"And how does your daughter react?" I asked.

"She just doesn't listen to reason. She'll climb under the covers or put her hands over her ears. Or she'll get even louder and more upset. Last week it was so bad that I canceled my plans with Carlos and sent him and the baby-sitter home. Usually I go out, but then I feel so guilty that I don't enjoy myself. I know that Claudia is having a hard time with the divorce, but I end up *furious* with her for being so controlling. That kid is a little dictator."

What is going wrong here? Can you identify Alicia's problem?

Reasoning with Kids?

Reasoning with kids sounds like a good thing for any enlightened parent to do. In practice, however, it usually boils down to trying to convince them to see things our way. Alicia communicates to Claudia that Claudia's anger and distress are "wrong," excessive, or uncalled-for. Alicia not only wants to date Carlos; she also wants her daughter to *want* her to date Carlos. She not only wants her daughter to cut out the rude behavior (which is certainly a reasonable request); she also wants Claudia to *like* Carlos and to think that he is a nice man. It makes perfect sense that Alicia wishes that this were the case. But it is not possible to change our children's thoughts and feelings. More importantly, it is not our job. Trying will only leave us feeling angry and frustrated. It will also hinder our child's efforts to carve out a clear and separate "I" within the family.

Why is Alicia having such a difficult time simply accepting her daughter's feelings of anger and sadness? Perhaps Alicia herself is anxious about going out, although she may not be aware of it. Perhaps she overfunctions or "rescues" when it comes to other people's feelings—especially those of her child. So many of us do this. As soon as our son or daughter expresses sadness, anger, hurt, or jealousy, our first reaction may be to rush in and "do something" to take it away or to make things better. The "something" may be to give advice, interpretations, or reassurance. We may try to change the subject or cheer the child up. We may try to convince our child that she or he doesn't, or shouldn't, feel that way.

Emotional overfunctioning reflects the fusion in family relationships. Family roles and rules are structured in a way that fosters overly distant fathering and overly intense mothering. If our child itches, we scratch. This togetherness force between mother and child may be so strong that many of us have difficulty achieving the degree of separateness that would allow us to listen to our children in an empathic, low-keyed way, inviting them to talk more and elaborate as they wish. When we learn to stay in our own skin and avoid assuming an overfunctioning or "fix-it" position, children—whether they are four or forty—demonstrate a remarkable capacity to manage their own feelings, find solutions to their problems, and ask for help when they want it.

What would you do in Alicia's place? Claudia calmed down considerably when Alicia was able to take the following three steps:

First, Alicia listened to Claudia's thoughts and feelings without trying to change them or take them away. She did not offer her daughter advice, reassurance, criticism, interpretation, or instruction. Instead, she made empathic, non-fix-it statements, such as: "It sounds like you are pretty angry that I'm going out tonight"; "You really don't like Carlos very much, do you?" Claudia felt reassured by her mother's calm, nonreactive listening, and she began to more openly express her anger, fears, and unhappiness about her parents' divorce. Alicia felt as though a burden had been lifted from her shoulders when she learned to listen to her daughter's problems without having to "do something."

Second, Alicia realized that it was her responsibility to make her own decisions about dating Carlos—or about anything else, for that matter—and that these decisions were not based on her daughter's emotionality. Alicia communicated that she respected her daughter's feelings and took them into account but that she would not make her decisions in reaction to her daughter's emotional outbursts. For example, Alicia would say, "I know you are having a hard time tonight, but Carlos and I are still going to the movies and then out to dinner. I will be home at about eleven-thirty, after you are asleep." And when Claudia said tearfully, "I hate him," Alicia simply replied, "I understand that." Claudia, like all children, was ultimately reassured to know that she could express the full range of her thoughts and feelings but that her mother was separate and mature enough to take responsibility for making her own independent, thought-through decisions, for herself and for Claudia as well. In the old pattern, Alicia would give in to Claudia and then angrily blame her for being manipulative ("That kid always gets her way!").

Third, Alicia took responsibility for setting clear rules about behavior and enforcing them. For example, throwing a tantrum was unacceptable behavior. If Claudia did this, Alicia would pick her up and take her to her room, where she would have to stay until she calmed down. Alicia also clarified that it was not acceptable for Claudia to continue to ignore Carlos whenever he spoke to her. "You do not have to talk to Carlos if you don't want to," Alicia said to her daughter. "But if he asks you a question, *tell* him if you don't want to talk about it instead of just ignoring him." For several weeks Claudia proceeded to say "I don't want to talk about it" every time Carlos initiated a conversation. Alicia decided that she could live with this behavior. Alicia also observed that the more she pursued her daughter to relate to Carlos, and the more Carlos attempted to move closer to Claudia, the more Claudia distanced. She and Carlos were both able to back off a bit and provide Claudia with the space she wanted. When Claudia no longer felt pressured to like Carlos or to feel close to him, she felt more comfortable and relaxed in his presence and in time she began to warm up to him.

With children, as with adults, change comes about when we stop trying to shape up the other person and begin to observe patterns and find new options for our own behavior. As we sharpen our observational skills, some patterns may be easy to identify ("I notice that the more I ask Claudia to discuss her feelings about the divorce, the more she closes up. But when I leave her alone and calmly share some of my own reactions to the divorce, she will sometimes begin to talk about herself.") Other patterns that involve *three* key people are more difficult to observe, as we shall see in the next chapter.

8

THINKING IN THREES

Stepping Out of
Family Triangles

Recently I visited my parents in Phoenix. I made this particular
trip because my father—who prides himself on having made
it to age seventy-five without even a sniffle—suddenly had a
heart attack. It was a wonderful visit, but after I returned, I
found myself feeling intense surges of anger toward my
children. During the next few days, Matthew began waking
up with headaches, Ben became increasingly rambunctious,
and the boys fought constantly with each other. My two
children became the prime target for my free-floating anger.

As I talked my situation over with my friend Kay Kent,
a sensitive expert on families, I began to make the connection
between my anger toward my children and my visit home
to my parents. The good time that I had had with my parents
was a reminder, not only of the geographical distance between
us, but also of how much I would miss them when they
were no longer around. On this particular visit, I could no
longer deny their age. My father was tired, considerably
slowed down, and easily out of breath. My mother, a spirited
survivor of two cancers and a recent surgery, seemed her
usual self; however, I was all too aware of her mortality.

Kay suggested that I address this new awareness directly with my children and parents, and so I did. At the dinner table the following night, I apologized to my whole family for being such a grouch and grump and I explained to Matt and Ben that I was really feeling sad following my Phoenix trip because Grandma and Grandpa were getting old and Grandpa's heart attack was a reminder to me that they would not be around forever and that one of them might die soon. "That," I explained, "is why I've been so angry." I also wrote a letter to my folks telling them how much I had enjoyed my visit and how, after my return home, I had come in touch with my concerns about their aging and my sadness about my eventual future without them.

What followed was quite dramatic: Both boys relaxed considerably and the fighting diminished. Each asked questions about death and dying and inquired for the first time about the specifics of their grandfather's heart attack and grandmother's cancer. I stopped feeling angry and things returned to normal.

The following week I received a letter from my father, who gave only a perfunctory reply to my self-disclosure by suggesting I not dwell on the morbid side of life. In the same envelope, however, he enclosed a separate lengthy letter to each of the boys explaining how the heart works and exactly what had happened in his own case. He concluded his letter to Matthew by directly addressing the subject of death. These letters, which were factual and warm, began the first correspondence between the two generations.

Underground issues from one relationship or context invariably fuel our fires in another. When we are aware of this process, we can pay our apologies to the misplaced target of our anger and get back on course: "I'm sorry I snapped at you, but I had a terrible day with my supervisor at work." "I'm scared about my health and I guess that's why I blew up at you." "I've been angry at everybody all day and then I remembered today is the anniversary of my brother's death." Sometimes, however, we are not aware that we are detouring strong feelings of anger from one person to another—or that underground anxiety from one situation is popping up as anger somewhere else.

It is not simply that we displace a *feeling* from one person to another; rather, *we reduce anxiety in one relationship by focusing on a third party, who we unconsciously pull into the situation to lower the emotional intensity in the original pair.* For example, if I had continued to direct my anger toward my misbehaving boys (who, in response, would have misbehaved more), I would have felt less directly anxious about the life-cycle issue with my aging parents. In all likelihood, I would not have identified and spoken to the real emotional issue at all.

This pattern is called a "triangle," and triangles can take many forms. On a transient basis triangles operate automatically and unconsciously in all human contexts including our family, our work setting, and our friendship networks. But triangles can also become rigidly entrenched, blocking the growth of the individuals in them and keeping us from identifying the actual sources of conflict in our relationships. The example below illustrates first a transient, benign triangle and then a problematic, entrenched one.

A Triangle on the Home Front

Judy is a real estate agent and Victor, her husband, is a salesman for the telephone company. On this particular day

Victor has a meeting after work and phones Judy to tell her that he will not be home until seven o'clock. Judy has been with the children all afternoon and finds herself tense and tired by the time the evening meal rolls around. She cooks dinner for the children, who, sensing her mood, act out more than usual, which only puts a greater strain on her. She cleans up, and watches the clock for Victor to come home. At seven-thirty Victor walks through the front door.

"I'm sorry I'm late," he says. "There was an accident on the road and I got stuck."

It is an entirely reasonable excuse, but Judy is furious. Not, however—as she experiences it—because of her *own* needs. She is not able to acknowledge that.

"I'm really upset!" she says, with intense anger in her voice. "Johnny and Mary [the children] have been waiting all day for you to come home. Now it's almost their bedtime. And I'm especially worried about Johnny. You've hardly been with him this week. He has been missing you terribly. He is a son without a father!"

What is happening here? The question of Victor's parenting may be a worthwhile subject for discussion, but it is not to the point. At this moment Judy is using the children as a deflection from an important issue between her and Victor. Victor, too, may have his own motives for colluding with this deflection.

Perhaps Judy feels that she has no right to be angry about Victor's late return. After all, the meeting was an important part of his job and the traffic jam was not his doing. Her belief that her anger is not rational, legitimate, or mature may prevent her from being able to articulate it, even to herself. Or it may be that the issue is a loaded one. Victor's lateness may touch on Judy's long-buried anger regarding the extent to which Victor is pulling his weight in the marriage.

If Judy and Victor have a flexible relationship, free from unmanageable levels of anxiety, the triangle will be temporary and of little consequence. When Judy cools off a bit, she will be able to share her feelings with Victor, including what a hard day she had and how angry and frustrated she felt when he did not return at five to offer her company and relief. But what if Judy does not feel safe speaking to Victor in her own voice? What if this couple is rigidly guarded against identifying the underground conflicts in their marriage?

Over time, a triangle consisting of Judy, Victor, and one of the children may become rigidly entrenched. Judy may find herself constantly blowing up at one of the kids instead of at Victor or she may intensify her relationship with Mary or Johnny in a manner that will help keep things calm on the marital front. This can happen in any number of ways: Mother and Johnny may form an overly close relationship that will compensate for a distant marriage and help keep father in an outside position in the family. Mother may complain to her daughter about her husband, rather than confining these issues to the marriage, where they belong. Or one of the children may become a major focus for concern, perhaps through the development of an emotional or behavior problem, thus drawing Judy's attention away from her own dissatisfaction in the marriage and perhaps enabling Victor and Judy to experience a pseudo-closeness as parents attempting to care for their troubled child.

The third leg of the triangle need not be a child. It could be Judy's mother, an in-law, or a person with whom Judy or Victor is having an affair. Triangles take on an endless variety of forms; but in each case, the intensity between Judy and a third party will be fueled by unaddressed issues in her marriage, and marital issues will become increasingly difficult to work on as the triangle becomes more entrenched. Of course, Judy's anger at her husband may be gaining steam from unaddressed issues with others, such as her own mother or father.

People of both sexes and all ages participate in multiple, interlocking triangles that may span several generations. But, as we have seen, women often have a greater, exaggerated fear about rocking the boat in an important relationship with a man. Thus, we are likely to avoid a direct confrontation and instead detour our anger through a relationship with a less powerful person, such as a child or another woman. How might such a triangle operate at work?

A Triangle on the Job

Melissa was a bright young woman who was appointed Director of Nursing in a small private hospital run almost exclusively by men. As it turned out, she was occupying a token position that afforded her little real authority. Month after month, Melissa sat in meetings where her contributions were ignored and where she felt increasingly powerless to influence institutional policy affecting the nursing discipline.

Melissa's sense of gratitude for being among the "chosen few," her dread of her own anger at male authorities, and her unconscious fear that greater personal clarity might lead to a confrontation that would lose her the approval of those in power—all combined to keep her from feeling angry and addressing issues directly where they belonged. Melissa's customary style was to behave deferentially to high-status males and to protect men in authority from the criticisms of other women. Perhaps this style played some part in her landing the director's position to begin with.

Melissa began to deal with her underground anxiety and anger in a triangular fashion. First she began to supervise her nursing staff very closely, moving in quickly at the slightest hint of a problem. Over time she became increasingly reactive to one particular nurse, Suzanne, who became the third leg of the triangle. Suzanne was an outspoken, highly competent young woman who was not particularly mindful of rules and paperwork deadlines and who easily voiced the anger at male leadership that Melissa could not. Melissa overreacted to any careless error that Suzanne made · or paperwork deadline that she failed to meet, and began to treat her as a "special problem" who needed to be watched. For example, Melissa wrote long memos to another of Suzanne's supervisors about Suzanne's late paperwork rather than express her concerns directly to Suzanne. As Suzanne's anxiety skyrocketed, she unwittingly escalated things further by running around and trying to form allies among her fellow nurses to join her in criticizing Melissa. Tensions between the two women continued to mount. Suzanne's late paperwork became a more serious problem and six months down the road Melissa fired her, with the seal of approval from her male superiors.

Melissa and Suzanne were involved in a triangle that began at the highest levels of the organization. The relationship between Melissa and her male superiors could stay calm and nonconflictual because the underground anger was played out lower down the hierarchy, in this case at Suzanne's expense. Melissa made no moves to empower the nursing staff within the organization, and this remained the unspoken and unacknowledged hot issue between her and the male authorities.

Was Melissa, then, the *cause* of the problem? Did it start with her? Of course not. If Melissa had been in an institution where women were truly empowered and where she, as a female, was not a numerically scarce commodity at the top, her behavior would have been quite different. In fact, research indicates that women who hold positions of authority in male-dominated settings are not able to clearly define their own selves or successfully identify issues common to women until the relative numbers of men and women become more balanced. No one person was to blame for the scapegoating of Suzanne, nor was she a helpless victim of circumstances who had no participation in her fate.

In the best of all possible worlds, we might envision separate, person-to-person relationships with our friends, co-workers, and family members that were *not* excessively influenced by other relationships. For example, our relationship with our mother and that with our father would not be largely defined by the fact that they were battling something out together. We would stay out of conflicts between other parties and keep other people from getting in the middle of our own fights. If we were angry at Sue, we would go to Sue about it and not complain to Sally about Sue. We would not detour anger and intensity from one relationship to another. That's the ideal. However, we achieve it only more or less. Triangles are present in all human systems. When anxiety mounts between two people or conflicts begin to surface, a third party will automatically and unconsciously be drawn in. All of us participate in numerous interlocking triangles we are not even aware of. Many of these are not particularly problematic, but one or more may well be. How do we get out of something that we may not even realize we're in?

Understanding triangles requires that we keep an eye on two things: First, what unresolved and unaddressed issues with an important other (not infrequently someone from an earlier generation) are getting played out in our current relationships? Intense anger at someone close to us can signal that we are carrying around strong, unacknowledged emotions from another important relationship. Second, what is our part in maintaining triangular patterns that keep us stuck? To find out, we must begin the complex task of observing our three-person patterns. Let's consider a key triangle in a family that was plagued by anger and anxiety on all fronts.

A MULTIGENERATIONAL TRIANGLE IN ACTION: THE KESLER FAMILY

"I'm here because I'm very worried about my son Billy," explained Ms. Kesler, who had called the Menninger Foundation to request help with her oldest son and to get some relief from her own feelings of chronic anger and stress. "He's always been a pretty good kid, but since third grade this year, he's been having school problems. Billy and his father are at each other's throats about it and their relationship is deteriorating. I've done everything I can to change the situation between Billy and his dad and to help Billy be more responsible at school. Nothing helps. I'm feeling angry at Billy and I'm also angry at my husband, John, who is taking a punitive approach with the boy. I tried to get John to come with me today, but he's not interested. He thinks that therapists are quacks and that this is a lot of bunk."

In the first few minutes of our first appointment, Ms. Kesler's view of the problem became clear. The "problem" in the family was Billy and Billy's father. If we could ask Mr. Kesler, he might see the "problem" as Billy and Billy's mother. It is expectable, predictable, and quite normal for family members to define a problem in this way. When we feel angry, we tend to see *people* rather than *patterns* as the problem.

Below is a diagram of the Keslers' nuclear family. Squares stand for males and circles for females. The horizontal line connecting a square and a circle indicates a marriage. Children are drawn on vertical lines coming down from the marriage line, in chronological order, beginning with the oldest on the left. We can see that eight-year-old Billy is the first-born child, who has a six-year-old brother, Joe, and a four-year-old sister, Ann.

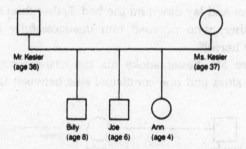

Mr. Kesler (age 36)   Ms. Kesler (age 37)

Billy (age 8)   Joe (age 6)   Ann (age 4)

Who Does What ... in Response to Whom ... and Then What?

What is the interactional pattern in the Kesler family that gets set in motion around Billy's school problem? All of us—

individuals and families—react to stress in predictable patterned ways. If Ms. Kesler is to use her anger as a guide for
changing her position in the family, her first task is to learn
to observe the current "stuck" patterns. When I questioned
Ms. Kesler about specific details, she described a sequence of
events that had occurred the previous evening:

Billy watched television after dinner instead of doing
some math problems that he had agreed to finish at this
time. Father noticed first and sternly reprimanded Billy for
behaving "irresponsibly" and "failing to meet his agreement."
Billy hedged ("I'll do it after this program is over") and his
father became angrier. Mother, who was doing the dishes
and listening from the next room, yelled from the kitchen,
"John, there is no need to be so hard on the boy. The
program will be over in fifteen minutes." Father yelled back,
"You stay out of this! If you didn't spoil Billy to begin with,
the situation in school would never have gotten this far!"
Mother and father continued to argue while Billy retreated
to his room and lay down on the bed. Father then distanced
from mother, who pursued him unsuccessfully and then
withdrew herself.

Before Ms. Kesler spoke up, the triangle consisted of
two calm sides and one conflictual side between father and
son:

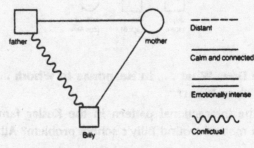

Distant

Calm and connected

Emotionally intense

Conflictual

When Ms. Kesler entered the interaction in a rescuing position toward Billy, she became the focus of Mr. Kesler's criticisms and the triangle shifted:

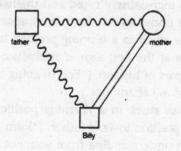

SCENARIO 1

This triangle would not necessarily be problematic if the pattern was transient and flexible. Let us suppose, for example, that the following events occurred later that evening: After Billy went to sleep, Mr. and Ms. Kesler talked together about their different perspectives on Billy's problem. They recognized that they had different opinions about the meanings of their son's behavior but were nonetheless able to reach a consensus on how to handle Billy that they both could support. Mr. Kesler then shared with his wife that he was upset about an incident at work and perhaps that was part of the reason why he had reacted so strongly to Billy. Ms. Kesler speculated that perhaps she was especially sensitive to his criticizing Billy because her own dad was always fighting with her older brother (also a first-born son, like Billy) and this had been very stressful for her. Mr. and Ms. Kesler would leave the subject of Billy behind as they moved on to talk about other issues in their personal or work lives or in their relationship together.

SCENARIO 2

But such flexibility did not characterize the Kesler family. Instead, Ms. Kesler was describing a repetitive pattern that was moving in increasingly rapid and intense cycles. When this family was under stress, the following occurred:

Father was stuck in a *blaming* position toward Billy. He became intense at the first sign of misbehavior or irresponsibility on the part of his son. ("You're going to get into deep trouble if you don't shape up!")

Mother was stuck in a *rescuing* position toward Billy and a *blaming* position toward father. ("John, that boy needs a little love and understanding from you, not an iron hand!") Sometimes she would adopt the role of the *mediating,* or *fixit,* person. She would offer both her husband and her son advice on how they might better handle each other and themselves.

Billy was stuck in the *underfunctioning* position in the family. He had already acquired the label "problem child" at home and in school and he was the overriding focus of parental worry and concern.

Last but not least, Mr. and Ms. Kesler were stuck in repetitive cycles of fighting over how to parent, in which Mr. Kesler stood for "law and order" and Ms. Kesler for "love and understanding." The emotional intensity of these fights deflected and obscured other important issues in their marriage and their personal lives.

WHAT NOW, MS. KESLER?

During the following weeks, Ms. Kesler learned to observe her own anger as well as the family's pattern of interaction around Billy's problematic behavior. Now she could more clearly identify her characteristic style of handling stress. She saw that she assumed a rescuing position toward Billy, a blaming position toward her husband, and occasionally a peacemaking or mediating position between Billy and his father.

Ms. Kesler also noted that her participation in the old pattern was not effective: Whenever she tried to come to Billy's defense, her husband perceived her as siding with Billy and turned his criticisms against her. Ms. Kesler was now ready to think about her options for moving differently.

Getting Out of the Middle

When we continue unsuccessful efforts to intervene in another relationship, we are part of a triangle. *The most difficult job that Ms. Kesler had before her was to let her husband and son fend for themselves and manage their own relationship without her.* Here's what she did:

First, she went to her husband and apologized to him for interfering in his relationship with Billy. She admitted that she might have made things worse by thinking that she had any answers or advice for either of them about their relationship. She empathized with her husband's worry about Billy and praised his involvement as a father and his efforts to help his son grow up to be a responsible person. She expressed confidence that he and Billy could work out whatever problems they had.

To her son, she said, "Billy, I realize that I've been getting exhausted by rushing in and playing the role of the American Red Cross when you and your dad argue. You're a smart kid and you know what gets your dad's goat. I am sure that you and your dad will be able to work things out together, and from now on you're on your own."

Next, Ms. Kesler did her best to *stay calm* and *stay out* when the countermoves came rolling in. Predictably, the other family members made some attempt to up the ante and reinstate the old triangle. Father took off his belt to Billy, whereas previously he had gone after his son only with harsh words. Billy ran to his mother, tearfully complaining about his father's cruelty. Even Billy's younger siblings got into the act. ("Mom, Dad's going after Billy again!") A typical "test" from Billy would go something like this:

> BILLY: "Daddy says I can't go to the baseball game tomorrow night, and I'm the catcher! Can't you make him change his mind?"
>
> MOTHER: "That's between you and Dad, Billy. Talk to him about it if it's bothering you."
>
> BILLY (*crying*): "But he doesn't listen!"
>
> MOTHER: "Well, Billy, this is between you and Dad to work out. You're both smart people. Try to work it out the best you can."
>
> BILLY: "Daddy isn't fair! *You* wouldn't make me miss the game!"
>
> MOTHER: "Daddy and I may set different rules sometimes. This is Daddy's rule, and whether you go to the game or don't go to the game is up to Dad. This is between you and Dad."

Although Billy tried to draw his mother back in the middle, he was enormously reassured by her new position. In a way, Billy was unconsciously testing out whether he truly had his mother's "permission" to have a separate relationship with his dad, or whether his mother needed him to be loyal to her, with the two of them subtly in alliance against a father labeled "unfair" or "incompetent." Through her new behavior, Ms. Kesler was letting Billy know that she did not need to keep up the old triangle, in which father would be on the outside. Billy could work things out with his dad without having to worry so much about his mom.

Maintaining her new position was anything but easy. "I get terribly tense when John and Billy go at it," Ms. Kesler explained to me. "When I hear John go on and on, I start feeling upset and ready to blow. Sometimes I go to the bathroom just to get away or leave the house to take a walk." Ms. Kesler was able to take this distance when she needed it, without criticizing her husband. In a calm, nonblaming manner she explained to him, "When you and Billy start getting riled up, I sometimes react by getting uncomfortable and upset. I'm not sure what my reaction is about, but when I start to feel this way, I may leave the room or take a walk because that helps." She made it clear to her husband that she took responsibility for her own feelings and reactions and she was not blaming him for "causing" her discomfort. Throughout the process, Ms. Kesler conveyed confidence that her husband and son could take care of their own relationship without her help.

But what if Ms. Kesler believes that her husband might physically abuse their son? Obviously, she will need to take a firm position against violence and protect Billy as best she can, even if this means calling the police. However, violence will be least likely to occur if she can do this without reinstating the old triangle, because *triangles greatly increase the probability of escalating aggression.* For example, she might say to her husband (ideally, at a relatively calm moment): "I need to tell you that I have a real fear that things between you and Billy will heat up to the point where he gets injured. I know that I can't solve anything between the two of you, but I can't live with violence. If that happens, I will do whatever is necessary to separate the two of you." To Billy, she might say pretty much the same thing: "I know that in the long run you and your dad have to work out your own problems. But, as I told Dad yesterday, I will step in if I get worried that things are getting so heated up that someone might get hurt." Taking a responsible position with each party need *not* mean falling back into the old pattern.

What happened in the Kesler family as a consequence of Ms. Kesler's getting out of the triangle? Mr. Kesler became less reactive to Billy's problems and provocations. He moved in less quickly and intensely. Billy, in turn, began to take more responsibility for his own behavior and his school problems all but disappeared. The relationship between father and son was greatly improved. Does this sound like the Kesler family lived happily ever after?

Not exactly. First mother and Billy started to have open conflict in *their* relationship. Further, marital issues concerning closeness and distance surfaced between husband and wife. Mr. Kesler became depressed and called me for an appointment despite his disapproval of psychotherapy.

Why did this happen? Triangles serve to keep anxiety-arousing issues underground, and that is why we all participate in them. When a triangle is disrupted and we begin to have a person-to-person relationship with each family member, without a third party interfering, hidden issues surface. This is emotionally difficult, but it also provides us with an opportunity to stop focusing on others and look more closely at our selves.

LOOKING BACKWARD: OUR FIRST FAMILY

When things settled down with Billy, the next step for Mr. and Ms. Kesler was to turn attention to their families of origin and begin to gather some data about the past. When a child or spouse is underfunctioning and has become the primary focus of our anger, worry, or concern, it is helpful to take a look at the larger family picture.

A broad approach to the problem will help to shed light on a number of questions: Why was Billy targeted to become a "problem child" in this family, rather than his younger brother or sister? Why did family interactions suddenly heat up when Billy entered third grade? Why was Mr. Kesler so reactive to the issue of "responsibility" in his son? Why was Ms. Kesler so reactive to her husband and son's fighting? Why did Mr. Kesler become depressed after he and Billy resolved their former conflicts? Most important, what work can Mr. and Ms. Kesler do to best ensure that no one family member will seriously underfunction or become the "problem," as Billy did?

Let's take a look at an expanded family diagram of the Kesler family and gather a few more facts. If you are feeling ambitious, you may want to draw a diagram of your own family, including, if you can, at least three generations. The diagram of the Kesler family, on the following page, is incomplete, in order to keep it uncluttered and to highlight certain key points. A complete family diagram would include the dates of births, deaths, serious illnesses, marriages, and divorces and the highest level of formal education for every member of the extended family, for as far back as we can go. An X in a circle or square indicates that the person is dead. Two diagonal lines across a marriage line indicate a divorce.

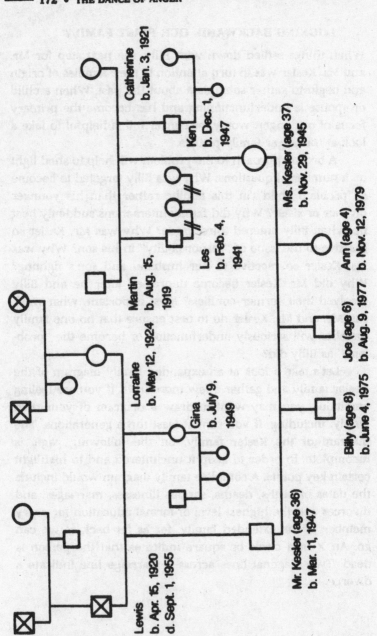

Catherine
b. Jan. 3, 1921

Ken
b. Dec. 1, 1947

Ms. Kesler (age 37)
b. Nov. 29, 1945

Les
b. Feb. 4, 1941

Ann (age 4)
b. Nov. 12, 1979

Martin
b. Aug. 15, 1919

Joe (age 6)
b. Aug. 9, 1977

Lorraine
b. May 12, 1924

Gina
b. July 9, 1949

Billy (age 8)
b. June 4, 1975

Lewis
b. Apr. 15, 1920
d. Sept. 1, 1955

Mr. Kesler (age 36)
b. Mar. 11, 1947

What does this family diagram tell us? Looking at father's side of the family, we see that he has a younger sister, Gina, who is married and has two daughters. If we do some simple arithmetic, we learn that Mr. Kesler's father, Lewis, was a first-born son who died at age thirty-five, when Mr. Kesler was eight years old. Mr. Kesler's mother, Lorraine, is the younger sister of a sister and did not remarry following her husband's death.

Looking at mother's family of origin, we see that she is a middle child. Her older brother, Les, is twice-divorced and her younger brother, Ken, is married and has one daughter. I learned from Ms. Kesler that Les is the "black sheep" in the family. In her words, "Les is an alcoholic who can always be counted on to screw up in business and marriage." Ms. Kesler's parents, Martin and Catherine, alternate between distancing emotionally from Les and bailing him out financially. Ms. Kesler is cut off from her brother and sees him only every few years at family gatherings.

Let us first examine father's side of the family diagram, with an eye toward linking the patterns of the past with those of the present.

Mourning a Father

When I gathered the above data during my initial appointment with Ms. Kesler, I understood why the relationship between Billy and his father had become intense and conflictual when Billy turned eight and entered third grade: Billy is now the age that Mr. Kesler was when he lost his father. In addition, Mr. Kesler is thirty-six years old, just past the age that his father was when he died. It is predictable that Mr. Kesler would have an "anniversary reaction" at this time and experience a reactivation of buried emotions that surrounded the loss of his dad.

Mr. Kesler did not directly mourn his dad or consciously experience the associated feelings of anger, anxiety, and loss as this anniversary date arrived. Instead, as is typical, he focused his emotional energy on a third party—his son— and became very reactive to any sign of trouble in Billy. *It is the intensity of our reactions toward another person's problem that ensures not only the escalation but also the continuation of the problem itself.* Billy's lack of cooperativeness increased in direct proportion to father's emotional reactivity (and mother's reactivity to father), setting a circular dance in motion.

Why did Mr. Kesler handle his anxiety by becoming focused on a child? This is a common way for mothers to manage emotional intensity and stress—as our social education actually fosters this child focus—but men are not immune from this triangle. Other triangular patterns might also have arisen. Mr. Kesler, for example, might have had an affair or left his wife at the time of this anniversary reaction. He might have distanced from her by becoming increasingly work-focused, which is a typical male pattern of managing anxiety. He himself might have underfunctioned and developed a new physical or emotional problem. He might have constantly found fault with his wife, leaving his children free from his emotional focus. We all handle stress in one or more of the above ways and, ideally, in more than one way. If the *only* way a family handles stress is to focus on a "problem child," the outcome will be a severely troubled child. If the *only* way a family handles stress is through marital fighting, the outcome will be a severely troubled marriage.

Why Billy?

Father and Billy share the same sibling position as first-born males. Father is thus more likely to identify with Billy than with his other children, to confuse Billy with himself, and to have more intense reactions to the strengths and weaknesses he perceives in his first-born son. Predictably, this might be the most problematic or intense relationship for Mr. Kesler, and the intensity would increase at a time of high stress. The fact that Mr. Kesler's own father was also a first-born further magnifies the emotional charge of Mr. Kesler's relationship with Billy. Birth order is an enormously important factor in determining how our parents perceive and label us and how we do likewise with our own children.

"Be Responsible, Son!"

Nothing pushed Mr. Kesler's buttons more than seeing Billy behave in a way that was not competent and responsible. Why?

The family diagram alone provides some good clues. At age eight Mr. Kesler lost his father and was left with his mother, Lorraine, who was the younger sister of a sister. What is known about the typical characteristics of a younger sister of a sister? As parents, often they are not comfortable taking charge, assuming a position of authority, and taking the initiative to do what has to be done. As a first-born child (and *son*), Mr. Kesler might have exercised *his* typical characteristics of "responsibility" and "leadership" at a very early age, perhaps trying to fill his father's shoes and help his widowed mother out.

When I met with Mr. Kesler, my speculations were confirmed. He had been a "little man" at an early age, and his own need to be a kid who could goof up and let others care for him was buried under a lifetime of overfunctioning and worrying about other family members. He was quick to react to the first sign of irresponsibility in Billy because Mr.

Kesler was *so* responsible as a child that he never really had much of a childhood. As he was later able to say to me, "I think I get so hot under the collar when I see Billy goofing off to have fun, because I'm a little jealous. After my father died, I stopped being a kid and became a worrier, long before I was really ready. My problem is that I feel *too* responsible for things."

"I Have a Problem"

Sometime later, during a week when Mr. Kesler found himself particularly reactive and angry in response to his son's casual attitude toward school, he took Billy on his lap and told him the following:

"Billy, this week I've been getting very upset and grouchy when I see you goofing up at school. I sure have been getting on your case. I think I figured out what my problem is. You know, Billy, when I was eight years old, my dad died and I was left without a dad. I felt angry and sad and frightened. And now that you are eight years old, like I was at that time, a lot of those old feelings are coming back. And sometimes the way that I deal with those feelings is to get on your back and fight with you so that I don't have to feel so sad about my own dad."

Billy looked at him wide-eyed. Then he said, "That's not fair! It doesn't make sense."

Mr. Kesler replied, "You're right, Billy, sometimes dads do things that don't make too much sense. I sure owe you an apology. It's my job to work on these old feelings I have about my dad dying. It's your job to decide what sort of student you're going to be in school. I'm going to do my best to try to work on *my* job and try to stay out of *your* job. I won't be successful all the time, but I'll be working on it."

"Does this mean that I can play with my friends and not have to do my homework?" asked Billy, with some mixture of anxiety and glee.

"Not a chance!" said Mr. Kesler, giving Billy a playful punch on the arm. "You know what the rules are, kid, and it's up to you to follow them. But you're going to have to decide what sort of student you'll be in school and I can't decide that for you, even though I may try sometimes." Billy said nothing, but several weeks later he began to ask all kinds of questions about Grandfather Lewis.

Taking the emotional focus off Billy did not mean adopting a "do-whatever-you-please-and-I-don't-care" attitude. Mr. Kesler's own style was to set pretty strict rules about the consequences of misbehavior. The degree of strictness or permissiveness will vary from family to family and is not, of itself, a problem. What is important is that Mr. Kesler enforced his rules without getting emotionally intense and blaming, and he made it clear to Billy that he (father) was dealing with his own issues and problems. It is also crucial that each parent support, rather than undermine, the rule-setting of the other, even if they don't always see eye to eye.

Most of us would not think of sharing something personal about our struggles with our children, as Mr. Kesler did—or as I did following my visit to my parents in Phoenix. Yet, there is hardly a more effective way to break a circular pattern. We maximize the opportunity for growth for all family members when we stop focusing our primary worry energy and anger energy on the underfunctioning individual and begin to share a bit about our own problem with the situation. This involves a shift from "You have a problem" to "I have a problem." In time—after working on the task of mourning his dad and modifying his overfunctioning position with his mother and sister—Mr. Kesler was able to do more of this.

What about Ms. Kesler? As we look at her side of the family diagram, what predictions might we make about her relationship with Billy?

A "Black-Sheep" Brother

Billy is in the same sibling position as Les—Ms. Kesler's "black-sheep" brother, who has made countless "bad moves" with jobs and women. In this key family triangle, Les is in the outside, underfunctioning role. Both his parents are in a blaming position toward him, while his sister, Ms. Kesler, takes a distancing position from him and a "fix-it" role with her parents. At times of low stress, she gossips with other family members about Les and his problems, and at times of high stress, she advises her parents on how to handle him and then gets angry when they ignore her advice.

While the emotional cutoff between Ms. Kesler and her brother keeps the anxiety down in *that* relationship, it is re-energized in her relationship with her son Billy, partly because he is in the same sibling position as Les and also because he happens to possess some actual physical and personality characteristics that remind mother of her big brother. Often, the underground intensity from a cutoff is not re-energized until an anniversary date comes up—for example, when Billy turns twelve, which is the age at which Les began getting into trouble, or twenty-three, Les's age when Ms. Kesler cut off from him. In the Kesler family, the intensity between mother and Billy began to surface when Ms. Kesler got out of the middle of the relationship between her husband and son and things calmed down on that front.

To some extent, we are all prone to confuse our children

with ourselves and with other family members. We project onto our children who we are and what we unconsciously wish, fear, and need. This process of projection gains steam from our unfinished business with siblings and parents. If mother makes no changes in her own family of origin, her projections onto current family members may be especially intense. She may, for example, encourage Billy to be a star in the family—an especially good child who will show none of the black-sheep qualities that she sees in her brother or fears in herself. Or, she may anxiously worry that Billy will turn out to be an irresponsible and troubled child like Les and unwittingly encourage this behavior by the intensity of her watchful focus on it. Billy may sense that his mother needs him to be a certain way for her own sake, and proceed to accommodate to or rebel against her needs. In either case, both Ms. Kesler and Billy become less able to directly manage the challenge of their own personal growth.

Like her husband, Ms. Kesler had "homework" to do with her family of origin.

Over time, Ms. Kesler gathered more data about her mother's and father's families, which provided her with a more sympathetic and objective understanding of why Les (rather than she) was more likely to underfunction and live out the black-sheep role. She learned to observe the patterns and triangles in her family of origin, as she had in her current nuclear family, and she took steps to get out of the middle of the relationship between Les and her parents. She did this by maintaining one-to-one emotional contact with all parties, without advising, taking sides, or talking with her parents about Les's problems. To do this required her to initiate closer contact with her brother, and she began to gradually share with him more about her life, including her own underfunctioning side. Eventually, she became much less focused on and reactive to the behavior of her husband and son, and she no longer felt dominated by anger and worry in these important relationships.

What Mr. and Ms. Kesler both learned is that children have a remarkable capacity to handle their problems when we begin to take care of our own. The work they each did with their own families was like money in the bank for Billy and his two siblings, because children are the carriers of whatever has been left unresolved from the generations that went before. Talking about the fact that Mr. Kesler lost his father and Ms. Kesler was cut off from her older brother may seem a bit removed from the subject of women and anger. *Yet all of us are vulnerable to intense, nonproductive angry reactions in our current relationships if we do not deal openly and directly with emotional issues from our first family—in particular, losses and cutoffs.* If we do not observe and understand how our triangles operate, our anger can keep us stuck in the past, rather than serving as an incentive and guide to form more productive relationship patterns for the future.

Let's take a look at a simpler family triangle in order to review the major points we have learned about observing and changing three-person relationship patterns.

WHY CAN'T HE MARRY A NICE JEWISH GIRL?

Sarah's son, Jerry, turned thirty-four the very day that Sarah showed up at my office. "My son, Jerry, is dating a non-Jewish woman for over three years," Sarah explained. "This girl—Julie is her name—is not even good for him and she has terrible problems herself. My husband and I know that he will be unhappy if he marries her, but my son won't listen to reason." Sarah told me that she was very *worried* about Jerry, but even a casual observer could see that she was also very *angry*. In fact, an atmosphere of chronic anger and tension permeated their relationship.

Jerry, I learned, was the younger of two brothers and still living at home. Although he graduated with honors from college, he had since been shifting from job to job, and his lack of direction was a source of family concern. Jerry, then, was in an underfunctioning position in the family.

Sarah's story is more than familiar to us by now. She is engaging in increasingly intense efforts to change her son despite the fact that such efforts only help keep the old pattern going.

What is the pattern? According to Sarah's description of her interactions, she blames and then distances under stress. Sometimes she blames Julie ("She just doesn't consider other people very much, does she?") and sometimes she blames Jerry ("I think you are rebelling against your family rather than making a mature choice"). When Jerry comes to Julie's defense or to his own, Sarah fights and then distances. While this is going on, Jerry's father distances from both his wife and his son, and then later unites with his wife in their shared concern over Jerry.

Sarah describes herself as occupying the outside position in the key triangle between herself, Jerry, and Julie.

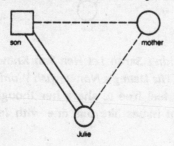

son   mother

Julie

When Sarah criticizes Julie to her son, she implicitly invites him to side with her against his girlfriend. Should Jerry go along with this, he and his mother would have a closer relationship at Julie's expense and Julie would temporarily occupy the outside position in the triangle.

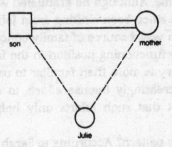

What more typically happens, however, is that Jerry comes to Julie's defense, which Sarah experiences as siding against her. At this point, conflict is likely to break out between mother and son.

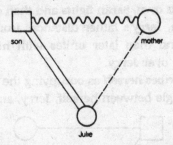

Why Shouldn't Sarah Let Her Son Know That She Does Not Approve of His Dating a Non-Jewish Woman? She should. Sarah ought to feel free to share her thoughts and feelings about important issues like this one with Jerry. She might, for example, let her son know what her problem is with the situation. Instead, she criticizes, advises, and blames. Now, nothing would be wrong with this if Sarah were satisfied with the situation. But she's not. As Sarah describes it, her interactions with Jerry frequently end in conflict and/or distance. The pattern has been going on for a long time, and Sarah is feeling angry and dissatisfied.

What Might the Payoffs Be for This Family in Maintaining the Status Quo? The old pattern will keep Sarah and her son stuck together in a close way (albeit negative closeness)—just like Maggie and her mother (Chapter 4), who fought about the baby in order to avoid negotiating their ultimate separateness and independence. The triangle between mother, son, and girlfriend here serves to reduce anxiety in the family by keeping other important issues between family members underground. It also protects Jerry and Julie from squarely identifying issues and conflicts in their own relationship.

What Can Sarah Do to Get Out of the Triangle? The three essential ingredients of extricating oneself from a triangle are: staying calm, staying out, and hanging in.

Staying calm means that Sarah can underreact and take a low-keyed approach when stress hits. Anxiety and intensity are the driving force behind triangles.

Staying out means that Sarah leaves Jerry and Julie on their own to manage their relationship. Therefore, no advising, no helping, no criticizing, no blaming, no fixing, no lecturing, no analyzing, and no taking sides in their problems.

Hanging in means that Sarah maintains emotional closeness with her son and makes some emotional contact with

Julie, as well. Sarah may temporarily seek distance when things get hot; but when "staying out" means cutting off, patterns tend not to change.

New Steps to an Old Dance

When Sarah was ready to get out of the old triangle, the following dialogue ensued:

"You know, Jerry, I owe you an apology for giving you such a hard time about Julie. What a terrible time I've had thinking about my son marrying a woman who's not Jewish—and it still is not easy for me. Sometimes I react with a lot of anger and hurt, and I guess you've been the target for that. But I'm beginning to realize that my feelings are my own responsibility and that it's not your job to ensure your mother's happiness. *Your* job is to find the very best relationship that you can for yourself—and only you can decide if that's going to be with Julie. Certainly, I'm in no position to make that decision for you or even to know what's best. I haven't even given Julie half a chance!"

Jerry stared at his mother as if she had just come down from another planet.

"Even though I've been on your back," Sarah continued, "I know that you're perfectly capable of making the best choice for yourself without my help. You know, I was just remembering something the other day. Before I met your dad, I was dating someone my parents didn't approve of. I never really stood up to them even though I was grown up and earning my own money. Do you know what I did? I would sneak out of the house and see him in secret! Later, when my parents disapproved so strongly of your father, we ran off and eloped!"

Sarah let out a big laugh and Jerry closed his mouth, which had been hanging open. He looked at his mother with curiosity. *This was the first time that his mother had shared something about her own experience as it related to their angry struggle.*

"Did *you* ever date a man who wasn't Jewish?" he asked, not knowing what to expect next.

"You know, I simply never considered it. I really don't think that it would have been possible for me. It just wasn't an option." Sarah became thoughtful and then continued: "But that was me, at another time. You and I are two different people."

Sarah felt wonderful after this talk, but that night as she got into bed, she was mildly depressed. She felt irritated with her husband, Paul, and provoked a fight with him, which eased her tension a bit about the change she was making with her son. What Sarah felt is simply the discomfort that occurs as we begin to move differently in an old pattern and navigate a more separate and mature relationship with another family member. As we have seen, pressures to reinstate the old pattern come from both within and without.

Two weeks later, Sarah encountered some tough tests of her resolve to move differently. Jerry dropped hints that he and Julie were talking about getting married. Sarah was able to stay calm and underreact. She did not hide the fact that she had always hoped for a Jewish daughter-in-law; however, her attitude conveyed respect for Jerry's judgment and recognition that choosing a wife was his job and not hers.

Jerry then began a new series of countermoves, as he started to criticize Julie to his mother. "Do you know, Mother, Julie's father had a birthday today and I couldn't even get Julie to call him or stop by." With increasing frequency and ingenuity, Jerry invited his mother to join him in criticizing Julie. Sarah bit her tongue so as not to bite the bait. Instead she said, "Well, you know Julie much better than I do. If that bothers you, perhaps you can talk with her about it and let her know your feelings." Or, "Whatever the problem is, I'm sure the two of you can work it out." Sarah herself was initiating more contact with Julie and was discovering things about her she genuinely liked and respected.

Had Sarah joined with her son in criticizing Julie, she would have reinstated the old triangle. The only difference would be that Julie, not Sarah, would occupy the outside position. People would change their positions in the triangle, but the triangle itself would remain unchanged. Anxiety would be reduced, but at the expense of each participant's ability to identify and negotiate issues with other parties.

If triangles keep underlying issues in each two-person relationship from surfacing, what happens when a triangle breaks up? Here is a brief look at some of the changes that had occurred in this family eight months later as a result of Sarah's extricating herself from a key triangle:

Jerry and Julie

Jerry and Julie were aware of some significant difficulties in their relationship and Jerry was expressing genuine uncertainty about whether Julie was the woman he wanted to marry. His critical feelings about Julie and his *own* ambivalence about marrying outside his religion had previously been held in check by the old pattern in which mother criticized Julie and he was free to come to her defense.

It was predictable that when Sarah got out of the middle of this relationship and gave Jerry her blessings to do the very best for himself, the real issues between Jerry and Julie would surface. If their relationship had been on firmer ground, it might well have been strengthened at this point. Apparently this was not the case.

Sarah and Jerry

The relationship between Sarah and her son became calmer and more open as Sarah became genuinely less reactive to her son's relationship with Julie. With the intense focus off this third party, the important issue of negotiating separateness and independence surfaced between her and Jerry. During one of our sessions together, Sarah said to me for the first time, "Julie or no Julie, I'm beginning to think that Jerry is having a hard time leaving home. What is a grown man doing still living with his parents? I find myself wondering if there's some connection between *his* problem leaving home and *my* problem letting him go. You know, I was never really very independent from my own mother. When she protested my marriage to Paul, we ran off and eloped and I didn't write to her for several months. I didn't have the courage to say to her, 'I love you, Mom, but I love Paul, too, and it's my life.' I just cut off from her and didn't face the issue."

Sarah and Paul

Paul was a quiet, withdrawn man who was not very comfortable with closeness. The mother-son-girlfriend triangle served him well because it basically left him out of this intense family dynamic and kept him and his wife focused on *parental* rather than *marital* issues. When Sarah stopped focusing her major "worry energy" on her son, she and Paul came face to face with the distance and dissatisfaction that each of them experienced in their marriage, and they were forced to pay closer attention to their own relationship. As a consequence, Sarah and Paul informed Jerry that he was to move out because they were getting older and wanted to enjoy some time and space for themselves. Jerry did find his own apartment, but he still attempted to hang on harder to test out whether his parents really meant business. When Jerry learned that they had no plans to take him back in and that they were managing just fine without him, he began to put his energy into coming to grips with his own pattern of multiple failures at work and in relationships.

Focusing on a "problem child" can work like magic to deflect awareness away from a potentially troubled marriage or a difficult emotional issue we may have with a parent or grandparent. Children have a radarlike sensitivity to the quality of their parents' lives and they may unconsciously try to help the family out through their own underfunctioning behavior. The "difficult child" is often doing his or her very best to solve a problem for the family and keep anxiety-arousing issues from coming out in the open.

Sarah and Sarah

Sarah's focus on Jerry and Julie also protected her from thinking about her own life goals. When she removed herself from the old triangle, she was suddenly confronted by some serious questions: What were her current priorities? What goals did she want to pursue at this point in her life? Sarah came face to face with her own self. How easy it is to avoid this challenge of self-confrontation by keeping our emotional energy narrowly focused on men and children, just as society encourages us to do.

If you are directing your primary emotional energy toward an underfunctioning family member, have you ever wondered where all that worry energy or anger energy would go if that individual was off the map? When Sarah stopped busying herself with her son's life, she began to worry about her own. Jerry, in turn, began to worry about his.

9

TASKS FOR THE DARING AND COURAGEOUS

Jog, meditate, ventilate, bite your tongue, silently count to ten . . .

There is no shortage of advice about what you can do with anger in the short run. Some experts will tell you to get it out of your system as quickly as possible and others offer different advice. In the long run, however, it is not what you do or don't do with your anger at a particular moment that counts. The important issue is whether, over time, you can use your anger as an incentive to achieve greater self-clarity and discover new ways to navigate old relationships. *We have seen how getting angry gets us nowhere if we unwittingly perpetuate the old patterns from which our anger springs.*

If you are serious about making a change in a relationship, you may want to read this book more than once. The important how-to-do-it lessons are contained in each woman's story. It is up to you to connect these with your own life. The patterns I have described are universal among women and you have undoubtedly recognized yourself many times. Nonetheless, you may initially feel discouraged when you try to move differently in *your* relationships. When you are *in* the dance, it is especially difficult to observe the broader pattern and change your own part. In this chapter I will suggest a few tasks to help you review some of what you have learned, add to your understanding of triangles and circular dances, and test out your ability to move differently in relationships. You may want to get together with a friend or form a group with other women who have read this book and who share your new vocabulary and insights.

PRACTICING OBSERVATION

Begin to observe your characteristic style of managing anger. Do you turn anger into tears, hurt, and self-doubt, as Karen did with her boss? Do you alternate between silent submission and nonproductive blaming, as Maggie did with her mother? We all have predictable patterned ways of managing anger and conflict, though they may vary in different relationships. For example, when conflict is about to surface, you may *fight* with your mother, *distance* from your father, *underfunction* with your boss, and *pursue* your boyfriend.

Give some thought to your usual style of negotiating relationships when anxiety and stress are high. My own pattern goes something like this: When stress mounts, I tend to *underfunction* with my family of origin (I forget birthdays, become incompetent, and end up with a headache, diarrhea, a cold, or all of the above); I *overfunction* at work (I have advice for everyone and I am convinced that my way is best); I *distance* from my husband (both emotionally and physically); and I assume an angry, *blaming* position with my kids.

If you are having difficulty labeling your own style, use the following as a guide:

PURSUERS

- react to anxiety by seeking greater togetherness in a relationship.
- place a high value on talking things out and expressing feelings, and believe others should do the same.
- feel rejected and take it personally when someone close to them wants more time and space alone or away from the relationship.
- tend to pursue harder and then coldly withdraw when an important person seeks distance.
- may negatively label themselves as "too dependent" or "too demanding" in a relationship.
- tend to criticize their partner as someone who can't handle feelings or tolerate closeness.

DISTANCERS

- seek emotional distance or physical space when stress is high.
- consider themselves to be self-reliant and private persons—more "do-it-yourselfers" than help-seekers.
- have difficulty showing their needy, vulnerable, and dependent sides.
- receive such labels as "emotionally unavailable," "withholding," "unable to deal with feelings" from significant others.
- manage anxiety in personal relationships by intensifying work-related projects.
- may cut off a relationship entirely when things get intense, rather than hanging in and working it out.
- open up most freely when they are not pushed or pursued.

UNDERFUNCTIONERS

- tend to have several areas where they just can't get organized.
- become less competent under stress, thus inviting others to take over.
- tend to develop physical or emotional symptoms when stress is high in either the family or the work situation.
- may become the focus of family gossip, worry, or concern.
- earn such labels as the "patient," the "fragile one," the "sick one," the "problem," the "irresponsible one."
- have difficulty showing their strong, competent side to intimate others.

OVERFUNCTIONERS

- know what's best not only for themselves but for others as well.
- move in quickly to advise, rescue, and take over when stress hits.
- have difficulty staying out and allowing others to struggle with their own problems.
- avoid worrying about their own personal goals and problems by focusing on others.
- have difficulty sharing their own vulnerable, underfunctioning side, especially with those people who are viewed as having problems.
- may be labeled the person who is "always reliable" or "always together."

BLAMERS

- respond to anxiety with emotional intensity and fighting.
- have a short fuse.

- expend high levels of energy trying to change someone who does not want to change.
- engage in repetitive cycles of fighting that relieve tension but perpetuate the old pattern.
- hold another person responsible for one's own feelings and actions.
- see others as the sole obstacle to making changes.

As we have seen, women are trained to be pursuers and underfunctioners with men except in the areas of housework, child work, and feeling work, where we may overfunction with a vengeance. Men characteristically distance under relationship stress and are excused, if not rewarded, for this style. Both sexes blame, but women may do it more conspicuously than men, and for very good reasons indeed. These reasons include our deep-seated anger about our culturally prescribed de-selfed and one-down position, combined with the taboos against recognizing and directly protesting our subordinate status, as well as our fear and guilt about the potential loss of a relationship. Barbara's blaming, underfunctioning position with her husband, who refused to "allow" her to attend the anger workshop (Chapter 2), was the first of many examples illustrating how blaming both protests and protects the status quo and how it differs from effectively taking a stand.

In thinking about your own patterns of response, remember that none of the above categories are good or bad, right or wrong. They are simply *different* ways of managing anxiety. You will have a problem, however, if you are in an *extreme* position in any one of these categories or if you are unable to observe and change your pattern when it is keeping you *angry* and *stuck*.

Begin to observe other people's characteristic style of managing anger and negotiating relationships under stress. How does their style interact with your own? For example, if you are an overfunctioner who lives or works in close quarters with another overfunctioner, you may admire each other's competence when anxiety is low. When anxiety is high, however, there may be some head-banging and locking of horns regarding the question of who's in charge, who's in control, and who has the right answers. ("Why did you go ahead and make a decision without consulting me!") The most likely candidates for this pattern might be two first-borns, especially if each has a same-sex younger sibling. If you are an underfunctioner in a love or work relationship with another underfunctioner, each party may be angrily accusing the other of not assuming enough responsibility or simply not doing enough. Perhaps the bills aren't getting paid or no one wants to get out of bed when the baby cries. When overfunctioners and underfunctioners—or distancers and pursuers—pair up, we have seen the kind of escalating pattern that gets set in motion under stress.

Get as much practice as you can observing the interactional sequences in which your anger is embedded. That is, when things get hot, step back a bit in order to keep track of who does what, when . . . and then what. Observing is a skill that is definitely worth developing before you attempt to perform a daring and courageous act!

CHOOSING A COURAGEOUS ACT

Make a plan to do something different with your anger in a relationship—something that is *not* in keeping with your usual pattern. Using the earlier chapters as a guide, *choose one small, specific task that you can calmly carry out and maintain when the countermoves begin and your own anxiety mounts.* Anticipate the other person's reaction and what you will do then. Even if you don't hold your ground, moving differently in a relationship is the best way to learn about your own self and the relationship. *Only after you begin to change a relationship can you really see it.* Here are some examples:

BREAKING OUT OF A CIRCULAR DANCE

If you are *pursuing* a distancer in a romantic relationship or marriage, carefully reread Chapter 3, which describes how Sandra broke out of the pursuit cycle with Larry. If you are *overfunctioning* for a child, reread Chapter 8, focusing on the changes that Mr. and Ms. Kesler made in their relationships with their children. If you are in an *underfunctioning* position with your partner, go back to Stephanie's relationship with Jane (Chapter 7) or Barbara's dilemma with her husband (Chapter 2). Decide in advance on a length of time (for example, three weeks) that you will hold to a new position and see what happens.

DEFINING A SELF

Think of one or two ways in which you can more clearly define who you are with family members, without criticizing or trying to change them and without becoming defensive when anxiety mounts. For some of us, sharing our competence and strength is a move toward defining a whole, more balanced self. For others, a more courageous move may be to let others know that we have been depressed lately and that we are struggling with work or with a relationship. Stating a clear difference of opinion and standing behind it in a relationship where we have been the accommodating partner is another significant move toward defining a self. The more we work on this task, the clearer our thinking about our anger and how best to make it work for us.

MOVING AGAINST CUTOFFS

If you have been emotionally cut off from a family member, it can be an act of courage simply to send a birthday card or holiday greeting. Keep in mind that people—like other growing things—do not hold up well in the long run when severed from their roots. If you are emotionally disconnected from family members, you will be more intense and reactive in other relationships. An emotional cutoff with an important family member generates an underground anxiety that can pop up as anger somewhere else. Be brave and stay in touch.

MOVING SLOWLY AND THINKING SMALL

If you are feeling angry, think very carefully about what new position you want to take before doing anything. By its very nature anger propels us into quick action, so guard against this. You will only fall on your face if you attempt to take a new position that you are not yet ready to take or that you have only casually thought through.

Alice was furious with an ex-roommate who had moved to Denver a year ago but was still storing her belongings in Alice's basement. There was plenty of storage space, but for personal reasons Alice wanted the belongings out and was becoming increasingly angry with the excuses coming from

Denver. ("I can't afford to do it right now." "The weather is too cold for me to move my stuff.") Alice had a long history of overfunctioning for her ex-roommate and rescuing her from stressful situations, so this scenario was nothing new.

After attending an anger workshop that I conducted, Alice enthusiastically rushed home and wrote the following letter to her ex-roommate:

> Dear Leslie,
> I am having a terrible problem with your belongings in my basement. It may be selfish or irrational of me, but for whatever reason, I just can't live with it any longer. If you do not get your stuff out within three weeks, I am giving everything to the Salvation Army.
>
> > Regretfully,
> > Alice

Leslie did not get her stuff out and Alice gave it to the Salvation Army. Leslie acted furious and despairing, and Alice, in response, became guilty, remorseful, and depressed. It is not that Alice did the *wrong* thing. The problem was that she too quickly defined and acted on a position that was not comfortable for *her*. Katy's struggle to set new limits with her elderly father (Chapter 6) illustrates that it often takes time and effort to define a position that is congruent with our beliefs and values—a position that we can stick to without suffering undue anxiety and guilt when the countermoves start rolling in.

Remember that women have a long legacy of assuming responsibility for other people's feelings and for caring for others at the expense of the self. Some of us may care for others by picking up their dirty socks or doing their "feeling work"; some by being less strong, self-directed, and competent than we can be so as to avoid threatening those important to us. Changing our legacy is possible but not easy. Think small to begin with, but *think*.

PREPARING FOR RESISTANCE

As you attempt to shift a pattern, prepare yourself not only for intense reactions from others but also for the *inner* resistance that you will meet. Elizabeth was a twenty-nine-year-old lawyer who had been chronically angry with her parents, who she felt kept her in a childlike role by refusing to be guests in her home. Whenever they visited her apartment, they would insist on taking her to dinner at a restaurant—and picking up the check, as well. When Elizabeth *herself* was ready for a change, she found a way to let her parents know that it was important to her to be a hostess to them on her own turf. She cooked them an elegant gourmet dinner that was an undeniable statement of her competence and adulthood, and to her surprise, both her mother and father praised her profusely.

The next morning Elizabeth woke up depressed and with a headache. She was beginning to mourn the loss of the old stuck-together bond with her parents that protected her from that funny feeling of separateness and aloneness that accompanies our moving from a fused to a more mature relationship. That same week her father fell on the golf course and ended up with his leg in a cast. You can't be *too* prepared for the power of countermoves, as well as your own resistance to change. If *you* are planning to initiate a more adult, person-to-person relationship with a family member, read the chapter about Maggie and her mother (Chapter 4) several times.

As you think about this book or discuss it with a friend, you will come up with your own ideas for a bold and courageous act. If anxiety about change is very high in your family or other intimate relationships, you may want to begin working on a relationship that is more flexible and less intense for you, perhaps with a co-worker, neighbor, or friend. Wherever you begin and whatever task you choose for yourself, here is a review of some basic do's and don'ts to keep in mind when you are feeling angry:

1. *Do speak up when an issue is important to you.* Obviously, we do not have to address personally every injustice and irritation that comes along. To simply let something go can be an act of maturity. But it is a mistake to stay silent if the cost is to feel bitter, resentful, or unhappy. We de-self ourselves when we fail to take a stand on issues that matter to us.

2. *Don't strike while the iron is hot.* A good fight will clear the air in some relationships, but if your goal is to change an entrenched pattern, the worst time to speak up may be when you are feeling angry or intense. If your fires start rising in the middle of a conversation, you can always say, "I need a little time to sort my thoughts out. Let's set up another time to talk about it more." Seeking *temporary* distance is not the same as a cold withdrawal or an emotional cutoff.

3. *Do take time out to think about the problem and to clarify your position.* Before you speak out, ask yourself the following questions: "What is it about the situation that makes me angry?" "What is the real issue here?" "Where do I stand?" "What do I want to accomplish?" "Who is responsible for what?" "What, specifically, do I want to change?" "What

are the things I will and will not do?"

4. *Don't use "below-the-belt" tactics.* These include: blaming, interpreting, diagnosing, labeling, analyzing, preaching, moralizing, ordering, warning, interrogating, ridiculing, and lecturing. Don't put the other person down.

5. *Do speak in "I" language.* Learn to say, "I think ..." "I feel ..." "I fear ..." "I want ..." A true "I" statement says something about the self without criticizing or blaming the other person and without holding the other person responsible for our feelings or reactions. Watch out for disguised "you" statements or pseudo-"I" statements. ("*I* think *you* are controlling and self-centered.")

6. *Don't make vague requests.* ("I want you to be more sensitive to my needs.") Let the other person know specifically what you want. ("The best way that you can help me now is simply to listen. I really don't want advice at this time.") Don't expect people to anticipate your needs or do things that you have not requested. Even those who love you can't read your mind.

7. *Do try to appreciate the fact that people are different.* We move away from fused relationships when we recognize that there are as many ways of seeing the world as there are people in it. If you're fighting about who has the "truth," you may be missing the point. Different perspectives and ways of reacting do not necessarily mean that one person is "right" and the other "wrong."

8. *Don't participate in intellectual arguments that go nowhere.* Don't spin your wheels trying to convince others of the "rightness" of your position. If the other person is not hearing you, simply say, "Well, it may sound crazy to you, but this is how I feel." Or, "I understand that you disagree, but I guess we see it differently."

9. *Do recognize that each person is responsible for his or her own behavior.* Don't blame your dad's new wife because she "won't let him" be close to you. If you are angry about the distance between you and your dad, it is *your* responsibility to find a new way to approach the situation. Your dad's behavior is *his* responsibility, not his wife's.

10. *Don't tell another person what she or he thinks or feels or "should" think or feel.* If another person gets angry in reaction to a change you make, don't criticize their feelings or tell them they have no right to be angry. Better to say, "I understand that you're angry, and if I were in your shoes, perhaps I'd be angry, too. But I've thought it over and this is my decision." Remember that one person's right to be angry does not mean that the other person is to blame.

11. *Do try to avoid speaking through a third party.* If you are angry with your brother's behavior, don't say, "I think my daughter felt terrible when you didn't find the time to come to her school play." Instead, try, "I was upset when you didn't come. You're important to me and I really wanted you to be there."

12. *Don't expect change to come about from hit-and-run confrontations.* Change occurs slowly in close relationships. If you make even a small change, you will be tested many times to see if you "really mean it." Don't get discouraged if you fall on your face several times as you try to put theory into practice. You may find that you start out fine but then blow it when things heat up. Getting derailed is just part of the process, so be patient with yourself. You will have many opportunities to get back on track . . . and try again.

Of course, most important of all is our ability to take responsibility for our own part in maintaining the very patterns that evoke our anger. Triangles are the most complex relationship patterns to get a handle on, so let's move on to review this subject.

NO MORE GOSSIPING

If you are angry at Sue, is she the first or the last person to know about it? If you are irritated by your father's behavior, do you deal with him directly or do you go tell your mother? Do you pick up your phone to call your daughter if you are angry with your ex-husband or your son? If you are angry that your co-worker is not doing her job, do you tell her directly or do you talk to her supervisor behind her back in order to express your "concern" about her work?

When two people gossip, they are having a relationship *at the expense of a third party.* That's a variation of the triangle. Because triangles lower anxiety, they are not necessarily problematic when they are transient and flexible. When a triangle becomes *rigidly entrenched* in a family, friendship, or work situation such that it interferes with healthy person-to-person relationships, then the connecting legs must be broken.

Triangles at Work

Suppose, for example, that you are angry at Sue at the office because she takes extra-long coffee breaks, and as a result, additional work falls into your lap. You try to talk to Sue about it, but her first response is to get angry and defensive. You then stop Sally in the hallway and invite Sally to agree with you that Sue is selfish and unfair. If Sally listens sympathetically, your anxiety diminishes. Perhaps this helps you to calm down and think more clearly about how to go back to Sue and manage your relationship with her. This would be an example of a transient triangle with no particular cost to anybody.

On the other hand, suppose that you and Sally continue to talk about Sue behind her back. This *deflects* you from dealing directly with Sue to work out the problem. You will feel closer to Sally because of Sue's outside position, and in this way you *detour* your anger rather than deal with it. If the triangle continues to persist over time, any one of the following is likely to occur:

- Sally's relationship with Sue will be influenced by the unresolved issues between you and Sue. For example, Sally may become more distant from Sue or more reactive to her. If Sally begins to like Sue, she (Sally) may feel disloyal to you.

- Sue's anxiety will rise and she may begin to under-function more at work. The more that two people talk about an underfunctioning individual (rather than each working directly on that relationship), the more that party will have to work even harder to gain competence.

- You will have increasing difficulty calmly and clearly negotiating your differences with Sue and maximizing the chances that the two of you will have the most comfortable work relationship possible.

Can't it be helpful to talk with Sally if you're angry with Sue? If your intention is to get Sally's perspective on your problem, and if Sally is able to provide it without taking sides, diagnosing, or criticizing either one of you, then a triangle will be avoided. More typically, however, we may begin with the virtuous intentions of clarifying the problem and trying to understand why someone is performing poorly, only to have our efforts turn into mutual criticizing sessions and the start of an entrenched triangle. It never helps anybody's performance to talk *about* them rather than *to* them. The more other people get involved in a conflict between you and another person, the less likely you'll be to resolve it with minimal anxiety and maximum clarity.

Here are a few do's and don'ts to help you avoid setting up triangles at work. The following advice holds for a friendship or a family situation as well:

1. *If you are angry with someone, that's the person you should tell.* Even if Sue is resistant, rebellious, or rude, she is still the person to deal with. And dealing with her doesn't necessarily mean venting your anger at her. It means making use of everything that you have learned in this book—not with a third party but directly with Sue.

2. *If you want to go up the hierarchy with your anger, make sure to go through the appropriate channels and be open about it.* For example, suppose that Karen (Chapter 5) asked her boss to change her job rating from "Very Satisfactory" to "Superior" and he refused. If Karen wants a third party to review her evaluation, she can find out what the acceptable procedure is and tell her boss that she plans to go over his head and why. If you are open about bringing in another party and you make sure to use the appropriate hierarchy, you may avoid forming a triangle that will escalate anger and stress in the long run.

3. *When you are angry, speak in your own voice.* Whether you are addressing a subordinate or a superior, don't bring in an anonymous third party by saying, "Other people think you're difficult to work with," or, "There have

been some complaints about your attitude." Nameless, faceless criticism increases anxiety and is neither fair nor helpful. If you have an issue with someone, use the word "I." ("I think ..." "I feel ..." "I want ..." "I am concerned ...") Let other people speak for themselves.

4. *Avoid secrets.* If you believe that it is your job to let someone (Esther) know that she is being criticized or gossiped about—"Esther, I want you to know that Tom is telling people that you are alienating customers"—understand that Esther may want to go directly to the gossiping party to clarify the problem. If you plan to swear someone to secrecy— "Esther, please don't mention anything to Tom or he'll know I said something to you"—better to say nothing at all.

5. *Don't become the third party in someone else's triangle.* If someone complains to you, you can listen sympathetically, but without blaming or taking sides. Often this doesn't occur to us, but with practice it's not hard to do. Remember that the best reason to avoid quickly becoming someone's emotional ally is that others have the best chance of working out their own anger and negotiating their differences if you stay calm, stay out, and stay emotionally connected.

This concerned but neutral position is, in the long run, the most supportive one to take, for it helps facilitate creative problem solving in others. Suppose, for example, that *you* are supervising Esther, and Tom is complaining to you that she is rude to her customers. You can first encourage Tom to deal with her directly. If Tom says, "But I told her twice and she doesn't listen," you might tease him a bit and encourage him to grab Esther by the collar and try a third time. Or when you see Esther, you might say lightly, "Hey, I think Tom has a gripe about you. Why don't you meet with him and straighten it out." If you can maintain a low-keyed, nonreactive, noncritical position and express confidence that both parties can work out their difficulties, chances are that Esther and Tom will do surprisingly well.

Triangles Begin at Home

You have just finished cleaning up your kitchen when the phone rings. It is your mother calling and she sounds quite worked up. "Let me tell you what your brother, Joe, is doing now! He's drinking again and he is about to lose another job. I wonder if he'll ever grow up and find himself." Or, "I'm so upset that your father will not pay any of your sister's college tuition. He's always been cheap, and since he married Debbie, the situation is even worse."

What do you do?

POSITION 1

You join your mother in her anger and criticalness. Or perhaps you listen sympathetically and then spend the next ten minutes talking with her about Joe's emotional problems or your father's penny-pinching.

POSITION 2

You come to the other person's defense: "Well, Mother, if you didn't keep bailing Joe out, he wouldn't be in such a mess." Or, "I really don't think you appreciate Dad's financial situation right now."

POSITION 3

You give advice, doing your best to stay neutral. You may attempt to explain the behavior of each party to the other or try to help your mother be more "objective" or "reasonable."

POSITION 4

You clutch inside and feel very angry at your mother for putting you in this position. You silently decide that you will avoid her as much as possible because she is so difficult to deal with. Perhaps you make plans to move to Alaska.

Can you find yourself in one or more of the above responses? Let's look at each position more carefully:

Position 1. Here, you have a closer relationship with your mother at the expense of either your dad or your brother, who is in the outside position in the triangle. You are allied with your mother in a blaming position toward another family member.

Position 2. Here, your mother will feel like the outsider in the triangle and she may redirect her anger toward you for not supporting her or not seeing the "truth" about your father or your brother. You are in a blaming position toward your mother and a rescuing position toward the other party.

Position 3. Here, you try to help both parties and be a therapist in your own family, which is not possible. Your mother will either ignore your advice or tell you why it won't work. You are in a "fix-it" or "peacemaking" position in the triangle.

Position 4. Here, you try to lower your stress level by avoiding your mother, resolving nothing in the long run and ensuring that the underground anger and intensity will emerge elsewhere. You are in a blaming and distancing position toward your mother in the triangle.

None of the above positions is inherently troublesome if

it is flexible and temporary. As the Kesler family illustrates, however, positions in a family triangle can become rigid and fixed. As *daughters*, we are frequently participating in a triangle with our mother and one other family member— our father (if our parents are legally but not emotionally divorced, this triangle may be especially intense), our mother's mother, or a sibling. As long as we take part in this triangle, our relationship with our mother is heavily influenced by *her* relationship with the other party. And our relationship with the other party is heavily influenced by that person's relationship with our mother. In fact, every relationship on all three sides of the triangle is influenced by issues from another relationship. When triangles heat up, a lot of anger and stress may fly around, but salient issues do not get clarified or resolved. Remember also, a triangle is not something that another person *does* to you. Triangles require the participation of all three parties, and any one party can get out of a triangle—that is, if you can tolerate the anxiety involved in the process.

If you can do some work on an important triangle in your first family, it will not only help you with your anger; it will influence every relationship that you are in. Do you want to give it a try? The first step, as always, is observation!

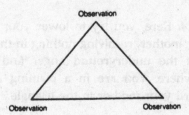

Observation

Observation   Observation

Sharpening Your Observational Skills

As you learn to observe your own position in a family triangle, you may want to diagram it. For example, when your mother calls and says, "Let me tell you what your brother, Joe, is doing now," you might participate in a triangle involving you, your mother, and your brother.

When things are calm in the family, you and your mother discuss Joe's problems (Position A). The relationship between your mother and Joe remains calm and distant because your mother is lowering her anxiety by talking with you, rather than dealing directly with her son. The relationship between you and your mother stays calm and close as you focus attention on your brother's problems instead of identifying and addressing issues in the relationship between the two of you. Here, the triangle looks like this:

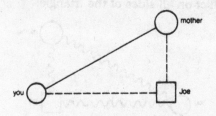

When stress increases, open conflict may break out between your mother and brother. You may then take a mediating position in the triangle, trying to be helpful to each party (Position C). You may say to your brother, "Mother really loves you." To your mother you may advise, "I think what Joe needs from you is a firm hand. It's not that he's bad; he's just testing the limits." Your relationship with both your mother and your brother intensifies, while the conflictual side of the triangle is between your mother and brother. Here, the triangle looks like this:

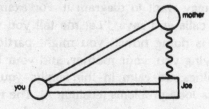

If tension escalates further, the triangle may shift again. Your mother may get angry at you for not seeing the "truth" about your brother, Joe may get angry at you for not taking his side against mother, and you may get angry at one or both of them for the way they are behaving with you or each other. All three of you are in a blaming position and there is conflict on all sides of the triangle:

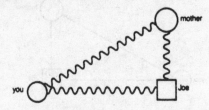

Can you now begin to identify your own position in a key family triangle? "Joe" may be your father, your grandmother, your cousin, or your aunt. If you're saying, "This doesn't apply to *my* family," keep thinking about it.

How would you respond to your mother's telephone call if your task was to move out of the triangle rather than participate in it? Close this book and get clear on what you would say, before reading further. If you feel stuck and unclear, reread Chapter 8.

Detriangulating Moves

When your mother calls to talk about Joe (or he talks about her), you can casually show disinterest. Remember that triangles are driven by emotionality and anxiety (our own included), so that the more low-keyed you can be, the better. You might say, "Well, I'm not sure what Joe is up to. Beats me what it's all about. I just don't know what to say. To change the subject, Mother, what are you up to lately?" When one party pressures you to give advice or take sides, you can do neither, and instead express your confidence in both parties: "Well, I don't have the slightest idea about what's going on, but I love you both a lot and I trust that the two of you can work it out." If your mother's focus on your brother remains persistent and intense, you might address the issue more directly in a nonblaming way. "You know, Mother, I feel kind of selfish about our time together and I'd like to use it talking about us and what's happening in our lives without bringing my brother in. I know you're struggling with him, but I don't have the slightest idea how to be helpful, and it takes time away from you and me. When I'm with you, I like to talk about you, and when I'm with him, I like to talk about him. Right now I'm much more interested in hearing about ..." In extremely rigid triangles, even greater directness may be required: "Mom, I just can't listen to you talk about Joe [Dad, etc.] anymore. I love you both and I need to work on my own relationship with each of you. I've no way to be helpful, and for some reason I just start feeling tense when you talk about him."

The exact words you choose are far less important than your ability to maintain a warm, nonjudgmental, nonreactive position. That is, you can calmly communicate that your relationship to both parties is important to you and that you have nothing to offer in the way of help, advice, blame, or criticism as far as their struggle with each other is concerned. Keep in mind that changing a pattern is never a one-shot deal but something we do over time—getting derailed when intensity mounts and then getting back on track again.

Do's and Don'ts

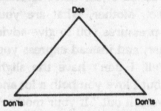

Here are some do's and don'ts to keep in mind if you are in the blaming position in a family triangle, as mother is in the above example. It's not only hard work to stay out of other people's conflicts, it requires just as much courage to keep other people out of our own. These suggestions can apply to any relationship network that you are in:

1. *If you are angry with one family member, put your emotional energy into dealing directly with that person.* If your reaction is, "But I've tried everything and nothing works," reread this book and think about new ways to move differently. If you feel stuck in an unsatisfying relationship and you want to talk about what is wrong with the other person, talk to someone outside the immediate family who does not have a relationship with the person at whom you are angry. It can be enormously helpful to share your struggle with a close female relative who may have been through a similar

experience, _if_ you can steer clear of a blaming position as you learn more about how she handled her own problem.

2. _Avoid using a child (even a grown-up one) as a marital therapist or a confidant._ Don't try to protect your children by telling them what's wrong with their father even if you are convinced that it will help them to know the "truth." Children need to discover their own truths about family members by navigating their own relationships.

3. _Distinguish between privacy and secrecy._ Each generation needs its privacy. Siblings need privacy from parents, and parents need privacy of their own. Secrecy, however, is a cardinal sign of a triangle when it crosses the generations. ("Don't tell your father that you had an abortion, because it will upset him too much." "Don't tell your sister that Dad lost his job, because she'll tell the neighbors." "Dad, I'm living with Alex now, but you can't tell Mom about it.") We may have the loftiest motives ("So-and-so just couldn't handle the information"), but the bottom line is that we are asking one person to be closer to us at the expense of another. If you are at the listening end of the secret-keeping business, you can let people know that there are certain secrets that you're just not comfortable keeping.

4. _Keep the lines of communication open in the family without inviting others to blame or take sides in your battles._ It's fine to tell your mother or your kids, "Yes, Frank and I are really having a hard time in our marriage now. We have many differences and we are struggling to work them out." This is quite different from inviting a family member to be your ally or take your side. Do your best to block other family members from getting involved in your battles. If little Susie says, "Daddy is just terrible to divorce you," you can say, "Susie, I am feeling angry with your father now, but it's

my job to work on that, and not yours. Your job is to work on having the best relationship with me and with your dad that *you* can."

All of the above are different reminders that every family member needs to have his or her own person-to-person relationship with every other family member—that is separate from your anger and your relationship issues with a particular party. You may be enraged at your ex-husband or black-sheep sister, but try not to discourage other family members from having the best relationship with that person that they can. Not only will others be *more* sympathetic with your situation in the long run, but you will be less likely to get entrenched in a bitter position in which your anger only serves to hold the clock still.

LEARNING ABOUT YOUR FAMILY

Katy's story (Chapter 6) is one illustration of how useful it can be, not only to share our problems with other family members, but also to solicit from them information about how they dealt with similar issues.

If you didn't do so when you read about the Kesler family (Chapter 7), *put together your own family diagram.* You'll be surprised at how many things—birth order of aunts and uncles, marriage dates, causes and dates of grandparents' deaths—you don't know. You may also be surprised at the connections you can make if you study this diagram. For example, you may notice that the year that you and your brother were constantly at each other's throats was the same year that your grandmother's health began deteriorating. Perhaps the fighting between you and your brother reflected the chronically high level of anxiety in the family at that time. The more you can enlarge your focus to the broader multigenerational picture, the less likely you will be to blame or diagnose yourself or others.

Many of us *think* we know our family background. Certainly we all have stories we tell about our family to other people. Such stories may elicit their admiration ("Your mother sounds like an incredible person!") or their anger ("How horrible that your father treated you that way!") or their pity ("What a terrible childhood you've had!"). We may tell these stories over and over during our lifetime, constructing explanations for things that we seek to understand. ("My mother always put me down; that is why I have such a bad self-concept.") However, these stories, including the psychological interpretations that we learn to apply to ourselves and others, are not substitutes for knowing our family in the sense of asking questions of our parents, grandparents, and other relatives and inviting them to share their experience. Most of us *react* to other family members, but we do not *know* them.

Give it a try. Use the diagram of the Kesler family on page 172 as a model for your own. The typical amount of information on a family diagram includes the dates of births, deaths, marriages, divorces, and illnesses, as well as the highest level of formal education and occupation for all family members, going back as many generations as you can. This may sound like a boring and tedious job, but you may be amazed at what you will learn about your family and yourself if you go about the task, perhaps reconnecting with family members along the way to get the information. Don't write off your "crazy Aunt Pearl" or "black-sheep cousin Joe" as sources of information just because they are the family underfunctioners. *Every* family member has a unique and valuable perspective and may be surprisingly eager to share it, if approached with genuine interest and respect.

Is learning more about our family truly a daring and courageous act? Yes, it is. It is not easy to give up the fixed notions that we have about our family. Whether we rage against one family member or place another on a pedestal (two sides of the same coin), we don't want the "stuck-togetherness" of our family to be befuddled by the facts about *real people*. In addition, we may not want to openly ask questions about taboo subjects in our family, such as our aunt's suicide or our grandfather's alcoholism. The problem is that when we are low on facts, and when important issues stay underground, we are high on fantasy and emotionality—anger included. We are more vulnerable to having intense reactions to any of the inevitable stresses that life brings—and to get stuck in them.

Remember that we all contain within us—and act out with others—family patterns and unresolved issues that are passed down from many generations. The *less* we know about our family history, and the *less* we are in emotional contact with people on our family diagram, the *more* likely we are to repeat those patterns and behaviors that we most want to avoid. Remember the old adage "What you don't know won't hurt you?" Well, research on families just doesn't support that one! Rather, it is the very process of sharing our experiences with others in the family and learning about theirs that lowers anxiety and helps us to consolidate our identity in the long run, allowing us to proceed more calmly and clearly in *all* of our relationships. "But my parents won't talk!" Well, gathering family data is a skill that can be practiced and learned; how you do it determines what you get.

The Courageous Act of Questioning

Pick an emotionally loaded subject in your family. The "hot issue" may be sex, marriage, cancer, success, fat, alcohol, or Uncle Charley. If it is a "hot issue" with your mother, for example, chances are you feel angry and "clutch" inside whenever the subject comes up. Perhaps the subject rarely comes up these days because you have taken a strong "I-don't-want-to-talk-about-it" stance.

Your courageous act is to stop reacting with anger long enough to open up a real dialogue on the subject by *sharing something about yourself* and *asking questions of others*. Your task in questioning is to gain some perspective on what has occurred in the previous generations that has loaded a particular issue to make it "hot." Only by gathering the broader family picture can you replace your angry responses toward family members with empathic and thoughtful ones. Let us take a couple of specific examples:

Suppose that one hot issue is your single status; every time you go home, your mother gets around to taking a jab at your unmarried state. What is your task?

First, calmly share something about where you stand on the subject. For instance: "Mom, I can see that you are concerned about my not being married. To tell you the truth, there are times when I feel concerned about it, too. At this point, I don't know if I'm scared of commitment, if Mr. Right just hasn't come along yet, or if I don't *want* to get married. I'm not clear about it yet, but I'm working on sorting it out." If you are an underfunctioner, guard against presenting your

problem as if you are just a bundle of weakness and vulnerability; if you are an overfunctioner, try not to make it appear
as if you have it all together and don't need anything from
anyone.

Second, open a dialogue with your mother about how
the issue of female singleness versus marriage has been
experienced in her family. *Block advice-giving and other "fix-
it" moves by clarifying that you are not interested in solutions
right now but in your mother's own perspective and experience
instead.* You might then ask your mother any number of
questions, such as:

> "I've been wondering, have *you* ever struggled with the
> question of whether marriage was right for you? And if
> so, how did you reach a conclusion?"
>
> "What worries do you have about me if I don't get
> married?"
>
> "If you yourself hadn't married, how do you think your
> life would have gone differently? What sort of work
> would you picture yourself doing?"
>
> "What was your mother's attitude about marriage and
> how would she have reacted if you had stayed single?
> How would your father have reacted?"
>
> "How did each of your parents react when Aunt Ruth
> didn't marry and worked on her career instead?"
>
> "Who in our extended family has not married, and how
> have they fared in your eyes?"

Questions like these will allow you to break the old
communication pattern, reconnect with your mother in a
more mature and separate way, detoxify the marriage issue
by getting it out from under the table, and learn more about

yourself and your family history. You may also learn about alternatives the family has found acceptable in the past, and prepare your mother for a greater range of outcomes in the future.

Now suppose that the "hot issue" for you in your family is your mother's ignoring your intellect and achievements and focusing on the successes of your brother. Again, your task would be to share some difficulty you're having in this area and then to ask your mother to help you out by sharing more about her own experience and perspective. What is most useful is to formulate questions that will allow you to get a picture of how the same emotionally loaded issue was played out a generation back with your mother and her family. For example, write your mother a letter explaining that it is difficult for you to work at succeeding and that the reactions of others are often *too* important to you. Then ask:

"How did *your* mother and father react to your talents and achievements?"

"Were you seen as smart in your family?"

"Which of your brothers and sisters were viewed as smart or not smart?"

"Did you ever think about going to college? What were your parents' attitudes about that?"

"If you had started a profession early in life, what career would have been your first choice?"

"Do you think you would have been successful at it? What might have stood in your way?"

"How was it decided that your brother was able to go to college and you weren't? What were your feelings about that?"

"What was it like for you to have so much responsibility in your family when you were growing up?"

"Did both your mother and father view themselves as smart and competent? Did they view each other that way?"

If you develop your skills in questioning, you will find that family members usually *do* want to share their experience if we first share something we are currently struggling with and assure them of our sincere interest in learning how they dealt with similar problems. *Parents and grandparents do not think to tell us their own experience. Instead, they tell us what they think we should hear or what they believe will be helpful to us.* Unless you are a good questioner, members of the previous generations are unlikely to tell you what it was really like for them.

A final postscript about fathers and mothers: If you take the initiative to move closer to your more distant parent (usually, but not always, your father)—by sharing more about yourself and asking more about him—you may find yourself feeling a bit disloyal to the other parent. For example, the distance that so often exists between us and our fathers may be the source of our angry complaints ("My father has no concern about me whatsoever"); yet we may actively (although unconsciously) go along with our father's "odd-man-out" position in a family triangle.

Be courageous! Defining a self rests on your ability to establish a person-to-person relationship with *each* family member that is not at the expense of another family member who is in an "outside" position. Also, keep in mind that if a parent reacts with increased distance to your initial efforts to be more in contact, this countermove is an expression of anxiety, not lack of love. Hang in, in a low-keyed way, and stay in touch. Remember, what is important in the long run is not the reactions you get from others but what *you* do—and how you define your own self and your personal ground in relationships.

EPILOGUE
Beyond Self-Help

"Defining a self" or "becoming one's own person" is a task that one ultimately does alone. No one else can or will do it for you, although others may try and we may invite them to do so. In the end, *I* define what I think, feel, and believe. *We* do not define what I think, feel, and believe. Yet, this lonely and challenging task cannot be accomplished in isolation. We can only accomplish it through our connectedness with others and the new learning about ourselves our relationships provide.

Self-help advice can be bad for our emotional well-being if it ends up conveying the message that major changes can be made easily or quickly—that, for example, if only you are motivated enough and follow this book carefully enough, you will achieve the happily-ever-after life. It is my hope that I have provided my readers with new perspectives on old angers; applying even one or two lessons from this book can make a significant difference in your life. But we both know that lasting change does not come about in a smooth, stepwise fashion and many of the women described in these chapters had the benefit of long-term psychotherapy to help them along.

Self-help advice can also be hazardous to our health if a "do-it-yourself" approach isolates us from other women. Throughout this book I have stressed the importance of learning about the experience of family members and sharing our own. Now I want to add that I believe it to be equally crucial for us to connect with the family of womankind, to share what it is really like for us, and to learn about the experience of others. It is through this process of reconnecting and sharing—of learning firsthand how we are similar to and different from other women—that allows us to go beyond the myths that are generated by the dominant group culture, transmitted through the family, and internalized by the self. Before the second wave of feminism, many of us suffered privately with our anger and dissatisfaction, maintaining a single-minded focus on the question "What's wrong with me?" Together with other women, however, we could stop blaming ourselves and begin to bring the old roles and rules into question.

Finally, self-help advice always runs the risk of fostering a narrow focus on our personal problems, to the exclusion of the social conditions that create and perpetuate them. This book has been about personal anger and personal change, but as feminism has taught us, "The personal is political." This means that there is a circular connection between the patterns of our intimate relationships and the degree to which women are represented, valued, and empowered in every aspect of society and culture. The patterns that keep us stuck in our close relationships derive their shape and form from the patterns of a stuck society. For this reason it is not sufficient for individual women to learn to move differently in personal relationships. If we do not also challenge and change the societal institutions that keep women in a subordinate and de-selfed position *outside* the home, what goes on *inside* the home will continue to be problematic for us all.

I believe that women today are nothing short of pioneers in the process of personal and social change. And pioneers we must be. For as we use our anger to create new, more functional relationship patterns, we may find that we have no models to follow. Whether the problem we face is a marital battle, or the escalating nuclear arms race, women and men both have a long legacy of blaming people rather than understanding patterns. Our challenge is to listen carefully to our own anger and use it in the service of change—while we hold tight to all that is valuable in our female heritage and tradition. If we can do this, we will surely make the best of pioneers.

NOTES

Chapter 1   The Challenge of Anger

1–2   Psychiatrist Teresa Bernardez was the first person to explore the powerful forces that prohibit female anger, rebellion, and protest, and to describe the psychological consequences of such prohibitions. See Teresa Bernardez-Bonesatti's "Women and Anger: Conflicts with Aggression in Contemporary Women," in the *Journal of the American Medical Women's Association* 33 (1978): 215–19. See also Harriet Lerner's "Taboos Against Female Anger," in *Menninger Perspective* 8 (1977): 4–11, which also appeared in *Cosmopolitan* (November 1979, pp. 331–33).

4   A well-known advocate of the let-it-all-hang-out theory is Theodore Isaac Rubin, author of *The Angry Book* (New York: Collier, 1970).

    For a critique of Rubin's theory, as well as a comprehensive and enjoyable book on anger, see Carol Tavris's *Anger: The Misunderstood Emotion* (New York: Simon & Schuster, 1982).

Chapter 2   Old Moves, New Moves, and Countermoves

21   The concepts of "underfunctioning" and "overfunctioning" are from Bowen Family Systems Theory. However, Murray Bowen discounts the far-reaching implications of gender and sex-role stereotypes. For a comprehensive review of Bowen's theory, see Michael Kerr's "Family Systems Theory and Therapy," in Alan S. Gurman and David P. Kniskern,

PAGE   eds., *Handbook of Family Therapy* (New York: Brunner/ Mazel, 1981), pp. 226–64.

22   In her book *Toward a New Psychology of Women* (Boston: Beacon Press, 1976), Jean Baker Miller discusses the subject of women as carriers of those aspects of the human experience that men fear and wish to deny in themselves.

23   On de-selfing and dependency in women, see Harriet Lerner's "Female Dependency in Context: Some Theoretical and Technical Considerations," in the *American Journal of Orthopsychiatry* 53 (1983): 697–705, which also appeared in P. Reiker and E. Carmen, eds., *The Gender Gap in Psychotherapy* (New York: Plenum Press, 1984).

23   While women have been labeled "the dependent sex," I have argued (ibid.) that women are not dependent enough. Most women are far more expert at attending to the needs of others than identifying and assertively claiming the needs of the self. Luise Eichenbaum and Susie Orbach have illustrated how women learn to be depended *upon* and not to feel entitled to have their own emotional needs met. See *What Do Women Want* (New York: Coward McCann, 1983).

29   For a more technical discussion of the forces of separateness and togetherness in relationships, see Mark Karpel's "From Fusion to Dialogue," in *Family Process* 15 (1976): 65–82.

32   Jean Baker Miller (op. cit., 1976) describes women's fears of hurting or losing a relationship as they move toward greater authenticity and personal growth.

34   On countermoves and "change back!" reactions, see Murray Bowen, *Family Therapy in Clinical Practice* (New York: Jason Aronson, 1978), p. 495.

Chapter 3   Circular Dances in Couples

43   Paul Watzlawick, John Weakland, and Richard Fisch have written about the "more of the same" (or "when the

PAGE   solution becomes the problem") phenomenon of human
nature. See Chapter 3 of *Change* (New York: Norton, 1974).

57   The marital pattern of distance and pursuit has been so
widely described in the family literature that it is difficult
to trace its origins. See especially Philip Guerin and Kath-
erine Buckley Guerin's article, "Theoretical Aspects and
Clinical Relevance of the Multigenerational Model of Family
Therapy," in Philip Guerin, ed., *Family Therapy* (New York:
Gardner Press, 1976), pp. 91–110. Also see Marianne Ault-
Riché's article "Drowning in the Communication Gap,"
Menninger Perspective (Summer 1977, pp. 10–14).

Chapter 4   Anger at Our Impossible Mothers

68   On the subject of emotional distance and emotional cutoffs
in families, see Michael Kerr's article on Bowen Family
Systems Theory (op. cit., 1981).

69   On mothers and daughters, see *Mothers and Daughters*,
by E. Carter, P. Papp, and O. Silverstein (Washington: The
Women's Project in Family Therapy, Monograph Series,
vol. 1, no. 1). See also (by same authors) *Mothers and Sons,
Fathers and Daughters* (Monograph Series, vol. 2, no. 1,
The Women's Project, 2153 Newport Place, N.W., Washington, DC 20037).

80   At the societal level, the same emotional counterforce
("You're wrong"; "Change Back!"; "Or else . . .") will occur
when a de-selfed or subordinate group moves to a higher
level of autonomy and self-definition. Feminists, for example, have been labeled selfish, misguided, and neurotic
and warned that if they persisted in their efforts toward
self-definition and self-determination, they would diminish
men, ruin children, and threaten the very fabric of American life. In both family and societal systems, it is a difficult
challenge indeed to stay connected and remain on course
in the face of countermoves that invite nonproductive
fighting and/or emotional cutoffs.

81   For a brief and highly readable summary on moving differently in one's own family system, see "Family Therapy with One Person and the Family Therapist's own Family," by Elizabeth Carter and Monica McGoldrick Orfanidis, in Philip Guerin's book *Family Therapy* (op. cit., 1976).

86   Maggie's story illustrates how we may resist change and sacrifice autonomy out of an unconscious belief that our further growth and self-definition will hurt other family members. It also illustrates that our resistance to change must be understood in the context of the powerful pressures against change exerted by the family system. For a more in-depth discussion of these concepts, see S. Lerner and H. Lerner's "A Systemic Approach to Resistance: Theoretical and Technical Considerations," in the *American Journal of Psychotherapy* 37 (1983): 387–99.

Chapter 5   Using Anger as a Guide

88   My thanks to Thomas Gordon for his pioneering work on "I-messages." I recommend *Parent Effectiveness Training* highly as a model of communication and relatedness that is applicable not only to parents and children but to adult relationships as well.

91   This vignette about Karen first appeared in "Good and Mad: How to Handle Anger on the Job," in *Working Mother* (March 1983, pp. 43–49).

95   For a more technical discussion of women's unconscious fears of their omnipotent destructiveness as well as the separation anxiety that leads women to transform anger into fears and "hurt," see Harriet Lerner's "Internal Prohibitions Against Female Anger," in the *American Journal of Psychoanalysis* 40 (1980): 137–47. Also see Teresa Bernardez (op. cit., 1978).

       Many psychoanalytic and feminist thinkers have discussed the irrational dread of female anger and power

PAGE   that both sexes share, dating back to our earliest years of helpless dependency on woman (i.e., mother), and have suggested that until parenting is shared in a more balanced way by men and women, such irrational fears may persist.

102   Hopefully my statement that we let go "of angrily blaming that other person whom we see as causing our problems and failing to provide for our happiness" will not be misinterpreted. Here and throughout this book, I am referring to nonproductive blaming that perpetuates the status quo; this must be distinguished from other-directed anger that challenges it. Obviously, the ability to voice anger at discrimination and injustice is necessary not only for the maintenance of self-esteem but for the very process of personal and social change as well. Teresa Bernardez (op. cit., 1978) has summarized the crucial importance of women gaining the freedom to voice anger and protest on their own behalf.

Chapter 6   Up and Down the Generations

112   The assumption that "Katy has the problem" is not meant to obscure the fact that personal struggles are rooted in social conditions. Ultimately, the question "Who takes care of elderly parents?" cannot be solved by individual women in their individual psychotherapies. A crucial arena for change is the creation of a cooperative and caring society that provides for human needs, including those of elderly persons. While social and political change is not the subject of this book, the sociopolitical context gives shape and form to our most intimate struggles.

113   For an excellent discussion of the problems as well as the special strengths that derive from women's assigned role as caretaker to others, see Jean Baker Miller (op. cit., 1976).

118   Gathering information about one's emotional legacy, including facts about the extended family, is an essential part of Bowen Family Systems Theory. In clinical work derived from this theory, one would not be encouraged

PAGE   to open up a toxic issue in the family or to move differently with a parent until one had obtained a calm, objective view of the multigenerational family process and one's own part in it. It is important to keep in mind that Katy spent quite a long time in psychotherapy, gathering facts and examining patterns in her extended family, prior to initiating the talk ("Dad, I have a problem . . .") with her father. For more about this process, see Carter and Orfanidis (op. cit.).

Chapter 7   Who's Responsible for What

125   Thanks to Meredith Titus for her ski-slope story.

129   How sibling position affects our world view depends on many factors, which include the number of years between siblings, and the sibling position of each parent. Walter Toman in his book *Family Constellation* (New York: Springer, 1976) presents profiles of different sibling positions, which are informative and fun to read despite the author's unexamined biases toward women, which color his presentation.

134   This vignette "Who's Doing the Housework?" first appeared in *Working Mother* ("I Don't Need Anything from Anybody," November 1984, pp. 144–48).

134–38   Lisa's problem with housework is another example of the inseparable nature of our personal dilemmas and the societal context. Were it not for the feminist movement and the collective anger and protest of many women, Lisa would probably not be struggling with the housework issue to begin with. If she felt exhausted and dissatisfied with her situation, she might have believed that she was at fault for feeling this way, and might simply have deepened her resolve to "adjust." As we do our best to define a position in a relationship, we are always influenced by predominant cultural definitions of what is right, "natural," and appropriate for our sex.

PAGE

142-47   My thanks to Katherine Glenn Kent for her excellent teaching on the fine points of the underfunctioning–overfunctioning polarity.

151   I recommend Thomas Gordon's *Parent Effectiveness Training* to help parents learn to listen to children without assuming a rescuing or "fix it" position. See especially his chapter on "active listening."

Chapter 8   Thinking in Threes

156   Much of what I know about triangles (a central concept in Bowen Family Systems Theory) I have learned from Katherine Glenn Kent.

161   See Rosabeth Moss Kanter's book *Men and Women of the Corporation* (New York: Basic Books, 1977) for an excellent analysis of tokenism and the special problems of women who are numerically scarce individuals in a dominant male work culture. For shorter reading, see Kanter's article "Some Effects on Group Life," in the *American Journal of Sociology* 82 (1977): 965-90.

162   My work with Mr. and Ms. Kesler illustrates an important epistemological shift toward systems thinking in the mental health field. This shift rejects the old linear model, which looks for a person to label as the "cause" of a problem (usually mother) and instead examines the reciprocal, repetitive, circular patterns maintained by all family members. Thinking in terms of family systems is a way of understanding people; it has nothing to do with whether a therapist sees one person individually or meets with a couple or family together.

171   For an informative videotape on how to construct a family diagram and its usefulness in understanding human behavior, see *Constructing the Multigenerational Family Genogram: Exploring a Problem in Context* (Educational Video

PAGE   Productions, The Menninger Foundation, Box 829, Topeka, KS 66601).

180   The psychotherapy described for the Kesler family is based largely on the theoretical concepts of Murray Bowen. While I have done my best to highlight key aspects of the process of change, it is important to note that this work is often a lengthy process requiring the help of a professional therapist who has worked systematically on his or her own family of origin.

180   For a videotape describing aspects of the clinical work derived from Bowen Family Systems Theory, see *Love and Work: One Woman's Study of Her Family of Origin* (Educational Video Productions, The Menninger Foundation, Box 829, Topeka, KS 66601).

Chapter 9   Tasks for the Daring and Courageous

205   Obviously, we may wish to support a coworker or join forces with other women to form an open alliance for a worthwhile purpose. Mara Selvini Palazzoli has written a brief piece on organizational systems that touches upon the difference between a functional alliance, on the one hand, and a covert coalition or triangle, on the other. This is a difficult distinction because in both family and work systems a triangle is invariably presented as an alliance with someone for a good cause and not as a coalition at the expense of another person. See "Behind the Scenes of the Organization: Some Guidelines for the Expert in Human Relations," in the *Journal of Family Therapy* 6 (1984): 299–307.

Epilogue

223   To keep informed about issues and events affecting women, I recommend subscribing to *New Directions for Women* (published since 1972), 108 West Palisade Avenue, Englewood, NJ 07631.

INDEX

Make
www.thorsonselement.com
your online sanctuary

www.thorsonselement.com

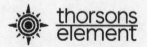

thorsons
element